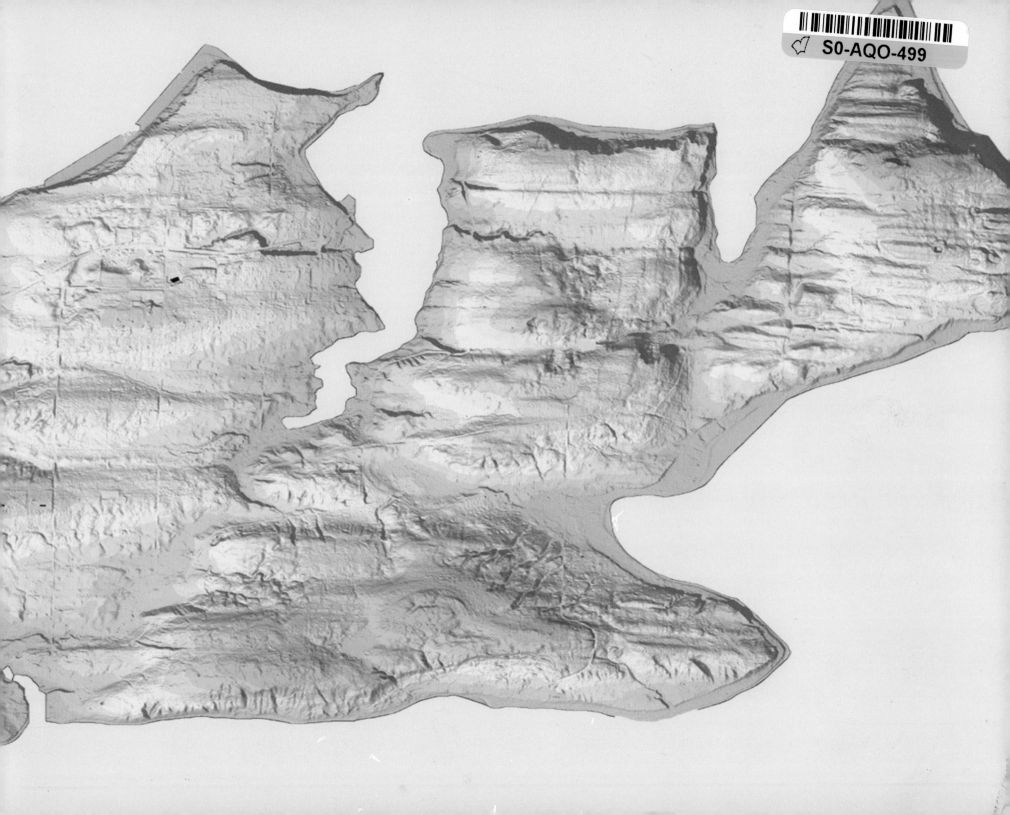

Sponsors

Picture Bainbridge would not have been possible without the generous sponsorship by the following Bainbridge Island individuals and organizations:

Bess Alpaugh

Thomas S. Alpaugh

American Marine Bank

C.V. Bucklin

Deschamps Realty

Tad Fairbank, Fairbank Construction Co.

Tom and Nancy Downs

Junkoh and Christine Harui, Bainbridge Gardens

Shirley A. Keith

Ed and Karen Kushner

Ocean Spar Technologies

Andrew and Marianna Price

Eddie Rollins

Jackie and Dean Scherer

Ken Schuricht and Mary Hall, Winslow Hardware

John Severt

Town & Country Market

Stuart and Janie Walton, Paper Products

Washington Mutual

West Sound Bank

Windermere Real Estate

Background: Charles Wilkes's map of the Northwest

Picture Bainbridge

A Pictorial History of Bainbridge Island

By Jack Swanson

Foreword by Ralph Munro

The Bainbridge Island Historical Society
Bainbridge Island, Washington

Published by The Bainbridge Island Historical Society
7650 NE High School Road
Bainbridge Island, WA 98110

© 2002 by The Bainbridge Island Historical Society
Printed in China through Phoenix Offset
By Jack Swanson, author for hire

Bainbridge Island Historical Society
    Picture Bainbridge, A Pictorial History of Bainbridge Island.
    Bibliography: p. 204.
    Includes index.
    1. Bainbridge Island—History.   2. Puget Sound area—History.
ISBN 0-9715147-0-4

    First edition

The publishers have generously given permission to use extended quota-
tions from the following copyrighted works:

    From *A History of Bainbridge Island* by Katy Warner. Copyright 1968 by
Katy Warner with printing rights given in 1978 to Bainbridge Island Friends of the
Library. Reprinted with permission of Friends of the Library.
    From *Port Madison, Washington Territory, 1854-1889* by Fredi Perry.
Copyright 1989 by Perry Publishing. Reprinted with permission of the author.
    From *Leaves from the LOG of William Bainbridge, Commodore, USN* by
Edward B. Doremus. Copyright 1996 by Edward B. Doremus. Reprinted with per-
mission of the author.
    From *Port Blakely: The Community Captain Renton Built* by Andrew
Price Jr. Copyright 1989 by Andrew Price Jr. Reprinted with permission of the
author.
    From *BAINBRIDGE through bifocals* by Elsie Frankland Marriott.
Copyright 1941 by Elsie Frankland Marriott, printed by The Gateway Printing Co.,
Seattle. Reprinted with permission of Bainbridge Arts and Crafts.
    From *Puget's Sound, A Narrative of Early Tacoma and the Southern
Sound* by Murray Morgan. Copyright 1979 by the University of Washington Press.
Reprinted with permission of the publisher.

The Dust Jacket

Captain George Vancouver's vessels HMS **Discovery** *and HMS* **Chatham,**
*anchored off Bainbridge Island's Restoration Point in 1792, prepare to
receive Native American visitors in this remarkable drawing by Bellevue
maritime artist Hewitt Jackson. Jackson spent several years researching
the details of the sturdy Whitbey colliers—coal carriers—that Vancouver
used during his four-year voyage of discovery.*

*Vancouver and his men spent ten days in the vicinity of
Bainbridge Island while they explored the Puget Sound region. The
Bainbridge Island Historical Society offers special thanks to Mr. Jackson
and Jim and Mary Dahlquist of Poulsbo, owners of the painting, for permission to reproduce it in this book.*

*The back jacket photo was taken from Bainbridge Island by
Patrick Tehan of* **The Sun** *in Bremerton and appeared on the back dust
jacket of the newspaper's book,* **Olympic Peninsula,** *published in 1994.*

Front end papers: Bare Bainbridge, *satellite image of Bainbridge Island
topography, courtesy of Kitsap Public Utility District No.1.*
Back end papers: *Hunting and fishing map of Bainbridge Island in the
1940s redrafted by Ron Munro, Bainbridge High School Class of 1953, from
an original by Ray Blair of Port Blakely.*

Contents

Ralph Munro

Ralph Munro, Bainbridge High School Class of 1961, served as Washington's secretary of state from 1980 to 2000. The Munros still maintain the family home on Crystal Springs.

Foreword

It was a warm spring day sometime in the late '50s. Thirty-five of us sophomores were crammed into a third-floor classroom at the old Bainbridge High School, listening to our Contemporary World Problems teacher trying to get us "fired up."

He spun around from the blackboard, threw his chalk at a buddy of mine in the second row, and asked, "Why would anyone want to live on this rock? The ferries don't run at night. The bridge leads to nowhere, the theater is still showing 'White Christmas,' and there's not a decent restaurant available until you get to Bremerton.

"This place is nowhere."

Slowly but surely, we started to fire back.

"Hey! We've got a great football team!"

"At least we have jobs in the summer. I'm going to Alaska this year and make a bundle."

"You know, the drive-in at Poulsbo has pretty good food, and, besides, the girls are cuter over there. . . ."

"Could be worse! Vashon doesn't even have a drive-in restaurant, let alone a movie. . . ."

Finally, one thoughtful girl in the third row said, "You know, I think it is 'quality of life.' It's peaceful here. We have plenty to eat. Our folks have good jobs. As kids, we have lots of fun, the schools are okay, and Seattle is close enough to obtain what the island doesn't have."

Quality of life. She hit the nail square on the head.

Take any Bainbridge family, shake it by the roots, and what you will find is that Bainbridge lifestyle ranks high in the list of reasons for coming to the island, raising a family, and seeking to spend your later years on the "rock."

Look at our history.

For hundreds of years, maybe thousands, our Native American families thrived on the clams, salmon, and berries that the island provided. Europeans arrived to seek the excellent harbors, tall stands of timber to harvest, and good soil to grow crops.

Asians and Pacific Islanders came to grow berries, to fish, and work in the shipyards. A walk through the island cemeteries quickly explains our rich ethnic background. And families still flock to the island for its beauty, serenity, excellent schools, a good-neighbor spirit, and "quality of life."

My grandparents arrived at Crystal Springs in the fall of 1890 and raised ten children on their small farm adjoining Port Orchard Bay. My dad spent the ninety-nine years of his life in that same location, living peacefully on the beach.

I once asked my dad and my old Uncle John, "If you could have any picture or image of what you have seen in your life, what would you choose?" My old uncle said he would love to have a picture of the Indians from North Puget Sound coming down the bay, heading for Ezra Meeker's farm in Puyallup to pick hops. He had seen this image as a boy.

The Native Americans, paddling their canoes, chanting, and singing, their dogs running on the beach ahead of them. An impressive sight for a young child of Scottish parents newly arrived in America.

As for my dad, he wanted a picture of the Great White Fleet steaming into Bremerton, something he remembered as a child.

And maybe you or your family have images of the island you remember, too. We hope that some of those images are included in this book. This is not just a volume of pictures for your coffee table. We hope it is a book of memories for your family as well.

All of us owe a hearty "thank you" to the Bainbridge Island Historical Society, the authors, editors, and many volunteers who put this book together.

Enjoy.

RALPH MUNRO

Preface

It takes a whole community to make a book like this. The project began in the fall of 2000 when Gary Loverich, president of the Bainbridge Island Historical Society, and I signed a contract to put together a pictorial history of the island.

This was to be a picture book, not a definitive or all-inclusive history of the island. We would use the immense photographic resources the society has collected as the result of generous donations from individuals and organizations as well as other sources not available to the public.

The text was to come from already published sources. To research everything from scratch would have taken many years.

More books probably have been written about Bainbridge Island history than about any other city in Washington. Only one is still in print, Katy Warner's delightful *A History of Bainbridge Island,* written to be used in the island's elementary schools.

Because of the efforts of the Bainbridge Island Friends of the Library to keep it alive, it remains the only island history available. Other books are difficult to obtain and contain only a few photos.

BAINBRIDGE through bifocals, the island's most comprehensive history, was published by Elsie Frankland Marriott in 1941. It contains fewer than a dozen pictures, and, alas, many errors.

Clearly, there was a need for a pictorial history of our island. The raw materials were there. But was the project feasible economically? Five years ago, the answer would have been no. But then the computer revolutionized the printing industry, and desktop publishing became available to everyone. The society's board weighed the risks and decided to go ahead.

As with any book, we had to decide when to begin and end.

Borrowing a page from James Michener, we began with the retreat

Bainbridge Island Review

Katy Warner, 1917-2002

This book is dedicated with love to the memory of Katy Welfare Warner who shared stories, advice, and encouragement.

of the glaciers. But where to end it? The Editorial Advisory Committee agreed that 1950 was as good a place as any because that was the year the island was a true island no longer. The Agate Pass Bridge changed Bainbridge Islanders' lifestyle forever. An era of physical separation from the rest of the United States had ended.

We will leave the last half of the twentieth century to others.

A small warning to the reader: Some of the things you will encounter may not be "politically correct" by today's standards. Some events we have included involved unseemly conduct and words that could be considered overly harsh or even racist by today's standards.

We have stuck with the standards of the time. This is our history. Unvarnished and unexpurgated.

We have many to thank for their help in producing this book. First among them are the staff of the Bainbridge Island Historical Museum, who had to put up with us constantly under foot, asking questions, taking up room in cramped quarters, and demanding ever more photographs and information.

Joan Piper, the society's director, was involved throughout the project, as were Erica Varga, curator, and Catherine Exton, museum assistant. Curator Tracy Vancura helped in the early stages.

Andrew Price Jr., author of the definitive history, *Port Blakely: The Community Captain Renton Built,* gave constant encouragement and helped root out our many boo-boos. Katy Warner, author of hundreds of newspaper columns as well as her book, *History of Bainbridge Island,* gave encouragement, enthusiasm, and many of her memories.

Port Madison resident Ed Doremus, author, printer, publisher, and binder of his excellently detailed *Leaves from the LOG of William Bainbridge,* shared his files and research on Commodore William

Bainbridge. His around-the-bay neighbor, Pete Seed, shared his home, many stories about early Port Madison, and memorabilia. Members of the Seabold Community Association shared the archives of the Seabold Community Center.

Ralph Munro and Reid Hansen, lifelong neighbors and friends, contributed family photos and childhood reminiscences of early Crystal Springs. Dozens of other islanders provided pictures and stories as well.

Richard Brown shared the archives of The Bloedel Reserve. Douglas Crist, editor of the *Bainbridge Island Review,* dug out mug shots of Katy Warner and contributed the final chapter of the book, the best piece ever done on the history of the Agate Pass Bridge. Joan Wilt and Wade Garretson shared rare pictures of early Wing Point

Gil Haight, grandson of Warren Gazzam, shared pictures of Gazzam and his imposing mansion at Crystal Springs. Howard Block of Bay Hay and Feed dug out an old picture of Rolling Bay's long-thriving mercantile center. Alexander Fisken opened his family album to provide early pictures of the Country Club.

Joel Sackett copied Hewitt Jackson's magnificent drawing of Captain George Vancouver's ships off Restoration Point. *The Sun* newspaper in Bremerton gave us permission to use the eye-popping photo of the USS *Nimitz* negotiating the narrow waters of Rich Passage. The Kitsap County Historical Society provided early pictures of Agate Point and William DeShaw.

We are indebted to the Seattle Museum of History and Industry for digitizing several images for the chapter on the evacuation of Japanese American residents in World War II. The University of Washington also provided several photos.

We had many fact-checkers. They included Sam Mirkovich Jr., Ed Doremus, Andrew Price Jr., Don and Donna Christopherson, Jim Dorsey, Bill

BIHS 1845

The Welfares at Home
Alfred Welfare, his wife Betty, and daughters Katy, second from left, and Billie, pose at their Port Blakely home. He grew up in Port Madison and worked as a steamer deckhand. Katy chronicled island events in thirty years of columns known as Katydids *for the* Bainbridge Review *under the byline Katy Warner.*

Weld, Charles Lindenberg, Alexander Fisken, Thomas B. Kelley, Gil Haight, Gerald Nakata, Junkoh Harui, Wayne Jacobi, Earl Hansen, Sarah Lee, and many others.

Members of the Editorial Advisory Committee—Reid Hansen, George Bussell, and Jim Usher—dug out photos and proofread pages. Christopher Charles made available several priceless maps and old books from his Winslow shop.

Lifelong Rolling Bay resident Bill Weld, official photographer for the Winslow shipyard during World War II, made available hundreds of original negatives from his personal archive on activities at the shipyard and at the Puget Sound Naval Academy, which was near his home.

We are blessed with many residents who participated in historical events and shared their memories and photographs. Among them are Dr. Frank Kitamoto, Junkoh Harui, Art Koura, Gerald Nakata, Ron Miguel, and several other members of the island's Japanese American and Filipino American communities.

Judy Richardson and Carolyn Hurst of Barker Creek Publishing in Silverdale spent many hours coaching me on book style and how to prepare a manuscript for the printer.

We owe special thanks to Pat Andrews, who spent hundreds of hours ferreting out my many mistakes. Not just once, but at least three times. Her understanding of the University of Chicago Manual of Style is unparalleled. She is the real editor of this book.

Most of all, I offer love and gratitude to my wife Cecelia and children Laura and Elliott, who gamely endured nearly two years of thrown-together meals and a grumpy old papa after many days and nights out in the barn where this book took shape. It has been a much longer process than any of us could have imagined.

Would we do it again? You bet.

JACK SWANSON

Strip Bainbridge Bare...

...as glaciers did tens of thousands of years ago, and you can see the deep scars left behind as massive ice sheets scraped across the earth's surface. The trenches etched into the island's surface running east and west in the center of the photo are High School Road. Highway 305 can be seen cutting from the northwest just south of Agate Point, across to Murden Cove, and then south to Eagle Harbor. This unusual computer image was produced from an infrared satellite photo.

Chapter One

In the Beginning

Exactly when was Bainbridge Island's beginning? Was it when the ice sheets retreated northward more than ten thousand years ago? When the first humans chased fish and hairy beasts south from the land bridge between Asia and North America? Or when European sailors anchored offshore while seeking a trade route to the eastern side of the continent?

The correct answer is probably that Bainbridge Island didn't become that until 1841 when Lieutenant Charles Wilkes named it so. But all of these answers bear some truth.

Geologically, the beginning was probably sometime during the last ice age that began 1.8 million years ago and ended about ten thousand years ago as the glaciers melted and exposed the Puget Sound region.

Elsie Frankland Marriott, author of *BAINBRIDGE through bifocals,* the first thorough history of Bainbridge Island, puts it more poetically.

> When the land was formed in the Puget Sound country, it was made a place apart—protected, favored, and beautified. Goodness only knows how long ago the Cascades to the eastward were thrust up out of the ocean—in Carboniferous times, the geologist tells us. Then the Olympics to the westward in the warm Mesozoic Age; the two ranges making a fortress for what was still to come. In that age palm-like trees and low evergreens grew and huge reptiles browsed beneath them. Then the Cascades were thrust still higher forming among the lesser peaks, Mount Rainier and Mount Baker to sentinel the sea, for only sea rolled between the ranges.
>
> Then from the north, glaciers crept down into the region, bringing with them vast burdens of rock and drift, the selected soil components gathered enroute. The centuries which followed have been called the Ice Age. Eventually the ice melted forming great rivers. Then the basin of the Sound was lifted, and after several fluctuations of land level in order to obtain exactly the right proportion of islands, rivers, and unsurpassed harbors, we find what it took many thousands of years to complete, A Charmed Land.

A charmed land. The land cradled between the mighty mountains was blessed with a year-round mildness of climate that was unique this far north of the equator.

"Yet on Puget Sound the elements are meted out with mildness the year round, and the fertile earth responds with a growth of luxurious evergreen. And flowers! Flowers are the fashion—all seasons," Marriott says.

As the glaciers receded, grasses, then trees, covered the scraped, barren landscape. Bainbridge Island still bears those long, deep scars. Drive west on High School Road from Ferncliff Avenue and every valley you hit is one of those island-long scars scraped out by one of those massive ice sheets. Bainbridge Island may well have been a peninsula before the sea level rose to isolate it from the mainland.

"This not-so-old island was likely an isthmus, an extension of a much different-shaped peninsula—barely recognizable by today's maps," says Gerald Elfendahl, self-described "historic map and story collector, beachcomber, stream scavenger and 'creek geek,'" in his book, *Streams of Bainbridge Island.* "Perhaps by six thousand years ago, the first marine water began to flow through Agate and Rich passages. The rising tidal waters began to flush one-time stream beds helping to form Fletcher Bay, Manzanita Bay, Port Madison, and what might be called 'Eagly' Harbor—one large inlet containing both Eagle and Blakely harbors."

Storm-driven rain and wind caused heavy erosion along the island's high bluffs on the eastern and northern shores, removing as much as a quarter mile of shoreline over a five-thousand-year period, Elfendahl says.

Another natural force also shaped our island. About one thousand years ago, several paleoseismologists say, an enormous earthquake occurred along a fault line that runs east and west across the southern tip of the island. The deep continental plates thrust the southern part of the island upward about twenty-five feet, exposing parts of the sea bed, including today's Restoration Point and Blakely Rock, making them part of the island's land mass, according to Robert Bucknam, retired former geologist with the U.S. Geological Survey.

The computer-generated map on page 10 shows the fault line running east and west just south of Blakely Harbor.

The map also shows how the land was shaped and scraped by ice flows over millions of years. In their *Historical Atlas of Washington,* James W. Scott and Roland L. DeLorme describe what was left behind.

> The Puget Sound region, located east of the Olympic Mountains, is an extensive lowland that is covered for the most part with a thick mantle of glacial till and glacial-outwash gravels and silt. The land forms there in general are more subdued than those to the east or west, and only occasionally are they spectacular.
>
> The gradients are gentler than in the regions on the east, west and south, but some scenic variety is provided by frequent changes in shoreline, which is interrupted by countless bays and many headlands and peninsulas.
>
> Offshore lie hundreds of islands, which range in size from San Juan, Whidbey and Bainbridge islands, many square miles in area, to tiny islets that show no more than a few square yards of exposed rock.

That's us. Thin soil, glacial till. Ancient peat bogs. Europeans who first visited the area remarked on the poor nature of the island's soil. About all it was good for was growing trees, which it did in abundance.

"For thousands of years the uses to which the land of Washington was put underwent hardly perceptible change as environmental conditions improved—or in some places deteriorated—following the retreat northwards of the ice sheets," Scott and DeLorme write.

"However, as population increases led to the spread of settlement, new demands were placed on the land and its resources. It is not too fanciful to suggest that when the first whites arrived in the Pacific Northwest the land looked little different from what it had looked like a thousand, even five thousand, years before."

The first settlers arrived in the region between ten thousand and forty thousand years ago, anthropologists say.

"Whether the date of the first migrations eventually turns out to be between fifteen thousand and nineteen thousand years ago, as many scientists think, or even earlier, there is plenty of evidence to prove the existence of the dry land which provided the route and a relative abundance of game—the woolly mammoth, the mastodon, and other large animals—which could have provided the motive for the Indians' passage from Asia eastward into North America," according to Scott and DeLorme.

"From the Bering Strait groups of Indian hunters followed herds of wild animals, moving slowly but inexorably—as climate changes dictated and new pastures beckoned—eastwards and southwards, eventually to populate both North America and South America."

The newcomers took three main routes, scientists say. The earliest was along the coast, probably down the inside passage between the Vancouver and Queen Charlotte Islands, feeding on sea mammals, fish, shellfish, and berries. Others migrated down the interior valleys between the Rocky Mountains and the Coast Range of present-day British Columbia.

Skeletal remnants of a twelve-thousand-year-old mastodon with a spear point embedded in its rib was found near Sequim in 1977. In the 1960s, a ten-thousand-year-old human skeleton was unearthed in a rocky cave near Marmes on the Snake River before the site was buried under the backwaters of Lower Monumental Dam.

More than five thousand sites of early habitation have been identified in the state, and only twenty-two had been studied in any detail by the end of the twentieth century, Scott and DeLorme say.

Bainbridge Island has hundreds of "middens," literally garbage dumps, along its shoreline. They indicate that, for thousands of years, visitors made camps to collect the island's shellfish and berries.

In short: It was a nice spot to visit, but who would want to live there year-round? Not the Native Americans. But one hundred and fifty years ago, a few pioneers decided that this rock wasn't such a bad place for full-time living after all.

That was the real beginning.

The Mysterious Picture Writing of Agate Point
Whether graffiti or the earliest writing found in the Puget Sound region, the art work on Agate Point's petroglyph was created hundreds or even thousands of years ago. By whom, no one knows. Bainbridge Islander John Rudolph, an amateur archaeoastronomer, theorizes that the rock served ancient residents as a solar calendar, enabling them to determine the first day of spring and fall. This charcoal rubbing was taken from the end of the rock, known as Haleets, by Gerald Elfendahl, former director and curator of the Bainbridge Island Museum.
(See page 51.)

13

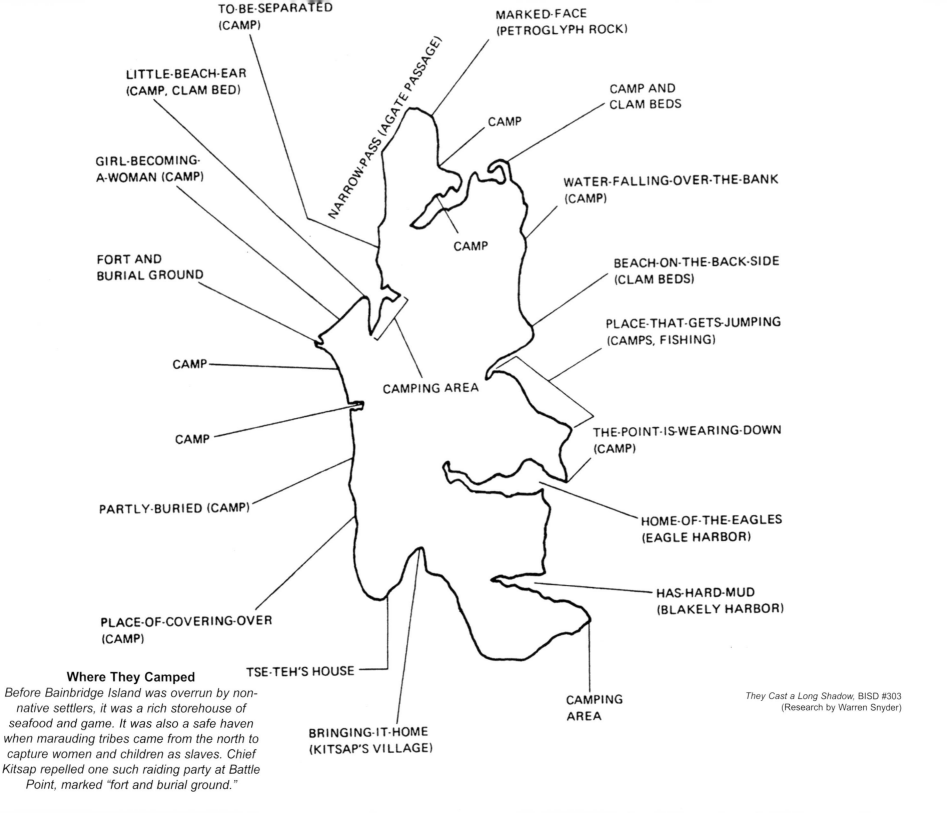

TO-BE-SEPARATED
(CAMP)

MARKED-FACE
(PETROGLYPH ROCK)

LITTLE-BEACH-EAR
(CAMP, CLAM BED)

CAMP AND
CLAM BEDS

CAMP

GIRL-BECOMING-
A-WOMAN (CAMP)

NARROW-PASS (AGATE PASSAGE)

WATER-FALLING-OVER-THE-BANK
(CAMP)

CAMP

FORT AND
BURIAL GROUND

BEACH-ON-THE-BACK-SIDE
(CLAM BEDS)

PLACE-THAT-GETS-JUMPING
(CAMPS, FISHING)

CAMP

CAMPING AREA

CAMP

THE-POINT-IS-WEARING-DOWN
(CAMP)

PARTLY-BURIED (CAMP)

HOME-OF-THE-EAGLES
(EAGLE HARBOR)

HAS-HARD-MUD
(BLAKELY HARBOR)

PLACE-OF-COVERING-OVER
(CAMP)

Where They Camped

Before Bainbridge Island was overrun by non-native settlers, it was a rich storehouse of seafood and game. It was also a safe haven when marauding tribes came from the north to capture women and children as slaves. Chief Kitsap repelled one such raiding party at Battle Point, marked "fort and burial ground."

TSE-TEH'S HOUSE

CAMPING
AREA

They Cast a Long Shadow, BISD #303
(Research by Warren Snyder)

BRINGING-IT-HOME
(KITSAP'S VILLAGE)

Chapter Two

The First Islanders

Nobody knows who discovered Bainbridge Island. But one thing we know for sure: It wasn't a white person. It was an Indian who lived more than five thousand years ago. That's how long we know that Indians have lived by Puget Sound. They may even have lived here long before that.

—They Cast a Long Shadow

We're all newcomers on this island. The Europeans who first visited Bainbridge Island 210 years ago were Johnny-come-latelies. The Americans of European and Asian ancestry who built sawmills and communities on these shores were intruders.

The island's first settlers built a major village on Pleasant Beach and had more than twenty campsites around the island in Eagle Harbor, Port Madison, Blakely Harbor, Manzanita Bay, Rolling Bay, and elsewhere.

By the time Europeans began nosing around and writing down permanent records, members of the Suquamish Tribe were using the island as a summer place, gathering shellfish, plants, and berries for the long winter days around the corner.

Chief Kitsap, the first tribal leader to greet Captain George Vancouver, had a summer residence in a village at Pleasant Beach and was camping with members of his tribe on what Vancouver would later name Restoration Point when the English anchored offshore.

Coastal dwellers from the Arctic to Oregon were highly advanced in watercraft and made war against each other from distances measured in hundreds of miles. Archaeological evidence also shows that hunters migrated south into present-day Washington by way of the long forested lowland valleys between the Coast Range and the Rocky Mountains. Native American tradition favors the water route.

Lena Hillaire, Chief Kitsap's great-granddaughter, told this legend before she died:

Way up north in Canada a long time ago some Indian braves were paddling a canoe along a river. They heard a deep voice saying, "Help, Help. A big storm has almost blown me down." The voice was coming from a giant cedar tree.

"If you will set me up straight and cover up my roots with earth so that I can keep growing, I will someday grow to be very tall with a huge trunk. Someday there will be another big storm, which will knock me down, and then you may make a giant canoe out of my trunk. You and all of your families can ride in this canoe away from the North Star, into the big water, until you come to a new land that will be like paradise. You and your families can live there happily forever."

So the Indians planted the roots under the earth and straightened up the huge cedar tree. Sure enough, many years later there was a big storm. When

BIHS 1754

Hard at Work
A Suquamish woman weaves a mat near a dugout canoe.

they went down the river again they saw their cedar tree on its side at the edge of the forest. They carved the big tree into a huge canoe and piled in all their families and tools and other things they would need in the new land. Then they came to a beautiful land, which we now call Suquamish.

Members of the Suquamish Tribe occupied the land west of what we now call Puget Sound. Their only enemies were tribes from the north, who would steal their belongings and carry their women and children off to become slaves. Europeans considered them lazy.

"The climate was mild, and they did not need much clothing, if any; the waters were full of fish and the forests overrun with game, therefore it was unnecessary to strive for food," writes Elsie Frankland Marriott. "They were bow-legged and bent from a lifetime of sitting tailor-fashion in their seatless canoes. This was all in decided contrast to the Indians east of the mountains, who were active, erect, and physically attractive. In the winter, woven garments of cedar-bark, or dog hair, or perhaps made of rat skins, were worn."

The Native Americans were excellent craftsmen. Their canoes were faster and sturdier than the small boats the white men used. Vancouver, however, belittled the island residents' abilities at building shelter after visiting their fishing encampment on Restoration Point. Vancouver wasn't aware this was a temporary camp. His party didn't see Old Man House, one of the largest man-made structures in the Pacific Northwest. Built at the site of the present-day town of Suquamish, it was made of cedar planks held up by massive posts and carved beams. The house served as the tribe's winter habitation, providing warm, dry shelter for as many as seven hundred residents. In 1841, members of the Wilkes Expedition said the building was 172 feet long and 72 feet wide.

Several explorers described the Suquamish and other residents of Puget Sound as being shorter than the Native Americans who resided across the mountains to the east. On the morning of May 3, 1841, a

INDIAN MAT HUT.

U.S. Exploring Expedition

day after Lieutenant Charles Wilkes had anchored in Discovery Bay near present-day Port Townsend, a large canoe came alongside his ship. Several Native Americans came aboard who spoke a few words of English, Wilkes wrote in his log.

. . . And we had occasion to notice the wide difference between them and the Polynesians, both in language and appearance. No contrast can be more striking than this. They seemed to have scarcely any idea of decency, and to be little less elevated in their moral qualities than the Fuegians [inhabitants of Tierra del Fuego].

The principal man of the party was dressed in a course coat of red cloth, with the Hudson Bay company's buttons, and corduroy trousers. He had neither shirt, shoes, nor hat, although the rain was falling fast. The others were habited in blankets or skins, and wore conical grass hats, resembling in shape those of the Chinese. They brought with them for sale some fish and a few furs. On the latter they appeared to set a high value, and were not a little disappointed when they learned that we had no desire to purchase them. They readily parted with their fine fish for a few fish-hooks and a little tobacco.

These Indians were short, thick-set, bow-legged, muscular, and seemed capable of enduring great fatigue. The most obvious peculiarity was the shape of their heads, which appeared to have been compressed, both before and behind, so as to give them the form of a wedge. Their cheek-bones were high, and their eyes, which were fine, were set wide apart: their colour was a light copper.

The oblique eye of the Chinese was not uncommon, and they had long flowing hair: aquiline or Roman noses were prevalent. Their countenances wore an expression of wildness, and they had, in the opinion of some of us, a melancholy cast of features. . . .

Wilkes discovered that the Indians were "of the Clalam tribe." The Clallams resided west of the Suquamish on the Kitsap and Olympic Peninsulas, and tribal members traded and intermarried.

"All the adults have their heads much flattened, which appears to be performed as it is among the more southern tribes, by compressing the frontal and occipital bones by several thicknesses of bark, until they become set, and the head takes a permanent shape," Wilkes wrote. "Their children seem to give them but little trouble: in their infancy they are tied to a piece of bark, which is hung to a tree or pole, where it is kept in motion by a string fastened to the toe of the mother, as is represented in the wood-cut at the end of the chapter."

The Clallams were considered by other tribes as being of lower social status. Tribes throughout the Puget Sound region practiced head-flattening to varying degrees. The Suquamish tended to flatten only a baby's forehead and not the back of the head. Native Americans that Wilkes and his men encountered had already adopted many implements from the Europeans, he said.

They also possess large sheath-knives, which they procure from the Hudson Bay Company, in exchange for furs, and from the same source they obtain blankets. For these articles the Company has a regular tariff of prices, which however, is not adhered to when a Boston ship arrives. . . .

The colour of the younger natives is almost white, so much so as to show the blush on the cheek; and some of the women would with difficulty be distinguished in colour from those of European race. The women are to be seen weaving mats, after the Chinese fashion, of bull-rushes, which they place side by side and fasten together at intervals. These are used, as has been stated, to cover the framework of their lodges.

The canoes of this region differ from any thing we had seen on the voyage. They are made from a single trunk, and have a shape that may be considered elegant, and which is preserved from change by stretching or warping by means of thwarts. The sides are exceedingly thin, seldom exceeding three-fourths of an inch, and they are preserved with great care, being never suffered to lie exposed to the sun, for fear of rents and cracks.

Many of Bainbridge Island's place names survive from the days

INDIAN MODE OF ROCKING CRADLE.

U.S. Exploring Expedition

Rocking the Cradle
A mother rocks her baby in a drawing by Alfred T. Agate, for whom Agate Passage is named.

of its earliest residents, point out the authors of *They Cast a Long Shadow.*

"Battle Point got its name from a fierce battle that was fought there," the book says. "The Suquamish were led by Chief Kitsap in that battle. They defeated Indians from Canada. They also won another battle where Port Madison is now."

Such battles apparently occurred frequently.

"There were other battles that the Suquamish did not win," the authors note. "Indians from Canada were their greatest enemies. They would swoop down from the north in their painted war canoes and make a surprise raid on a camp. They would take all the food and valuables. They would carry off women and children to be their slaves.

"The Suquamish would go up to Canada and do the same thing. They kept slaves too. Most of the Indian nations around here had slaves when the white people came. At that time white people had slaves too."

When Americans began moving into the territory in the 1840s and 1850s, the Suquamish accommodated them and even worked in the early sawmills. They listened patiently as white missionaries prayed for their souls and admonished them to adopt European-style habits.

On January 22, 1855, Chief Seattle, head of the Suquamish and Duwamish nations, signed a treaty with Washington Territorial Governor Isaac Stevens, recognizing the Suquamish Tribe's ownership of the Port Madison Reservation on the Kitsap Peninsula. It was the easiest treaty Stevens had ever negotiated.

A year later, the Suquamish didn't participate when tribes in the Seattle area tried to drive the settlers out. After the skirmish was over, the settlers forced the tribes to give up some of the land that had been theirs for thousands of years.

The Treaty of Point Elliott gave Bainbridge Island to the settlers.

Chief Seattle made clear, however, he was not happy with the terms.

The white chief says that Big Chief at Washington sends us greetings of friendship and good will. That is kind of him, for we know that he has little need of our friendship in return.

His people are many. They are like the grass that covers vast prairies. My people are few. They resemble the scattering trees of a storm swept plain.

The great—and I presume good—white chief sends us word that he wishes to buy our lands, but he is willing to allow us enough to live comfortably. This indeed appears just, even generous, for the red man no longer has rights that he need respect.

I will not dwell on, nor mourn over, our untimely decay, nor reproach our paleface brothers with hastening it, as we too may have been somewhat to blame.

In less than a decade, white settlers changed the landscape forever.

There is no quiet place in the white man's cities. No place to hear the leaves of spring or the rustle of insects' wings. But perhaps because I am a savage and do not understand, the clatter only seems to insult the ears. And what is there to life if a man cannot hear the lovely cry of a whippoorwill or the arguments of the frogs around a pond at night?

The Indian prefers the soft sound of the wind darting over the face of the pond, and the smell of the wind itself cleansed by a midday rain, or scented with a pinon pine. The air is so precious to a redman.

For all things share the same breath—the beasts, the trees, the man. The white man does not seem to notice the air he breathes. Like a man dying for many days, he is numb to the stench. . . .

All things are connected. Whatever befalls the earth befalls the sons of the earth.

MSCUA, University of Washington Libraries, NA1511

Chief Seattle

In the only known photograph of the great Suquamish leader, the chief closed his eyes.

Although he was the leader of a relatively small tribe, Chief Seattle was respected throughout the Puget Sound region.

"Old Chief Seattle was the greatest personality of all the Puget Sound Indians," writes Marriott. "The pronunciation of his name was hard for the English tongue; the name Sealth being no more accurate than the name Seattle, which was adopted at the suggestion of Doctor [David S.] Maynard, for the city across the sound. He was born about 1786."

"Seattle himself pointed out to Mrs. Maynard a place on Blake Island which had been a camping ground of his ancestors and told her that he was born there," wrote Cornelius H. Hanford. "When he was about six years old he was among those who gazed with wonder upon Vancouver's ships anchored near that island in the year 1792."

Hanford, who was raised in Port Madison and had met Chief Seattle as a boy, went on to become the last chief justice of Washington Territory's Supreme Court.

Samuel F. Coombs, one of the first school teachers on Bainbridge Island, interviewed several of the oldest Native Americans of his time as to how Seattle became head of so many tribes.

When Seattle was in his early 20s, Coombs learned, word reached the Puget Sound tribes that warriors from the mountain tribes were coming to raid the salt water tribes.

In previous battles, the marauders had carried off many of their people as slaves. Representatives of the coastal tribes met at Old Man House on Port Madison Bay.

"Many plans were discussed as to the best method of resisting the invaders. None of those suggested by the older men, however, was satisfactory and then the younger men were called upon for suggestions,"

Coombs said. "At length young Sealth, member of the Old Man House Tribe, presented his plan, and it was so well devised and so clearly presented that, without listening to any others, it was adopted and he was appointed to carry it out."

The warriors went up the Duwamish River in canoes and cut down a tree that fell across the river and capsized their enemies' canoes as they came down the fast-flowing stream. As a result of the victory, the tribes named Seattle their chief.

Hanford described the chief as "rather below medium height, round-shouldered, with spare limbs; his head was large and covered with long black hair, and although his features bore the prominent marks of Indian character, still, when speaking, his countenance beamed with an expression of pleasant dignity rarely met with among the race."

Seattle married twice and had two sons and five daughters. He owned six slaves. Seattle spent his last years in Suquamish and at Agate Point in a little house near that of his grand-daughter, Mary, and her husband, William DeShaw, who ran a trading post.

Seattle's health began to fail in 1866, Marriott writes. His last words were to request that George Meigs, owner of the Port Madison sawmill, visit him before he was buried.

Meigs closed the mill for the day and fulfilled the chief's request.

By the 1870s, the Suquamish had been largely displaced on Bainbridge Island and were confined to their 1,280-acre "reservation" around the original site of Old Man House.

A monument still marks Chief Seattle's grave on a hillside at the south edge of the town of Suquamish.

Mary Sam
Tribal slavery brought people of many tribes to the region. Longtime island resident Mary Sam, dressed in her mother's clothes, was a Klikitat Indian, stolen as an infant along with her mother by a Suquamish war party near Snoqualmie Falls. When Mary's mother died, her husband took Mary as his wife. Mary owned 10 acres near Port Madison and worked as a domestic for island families. She died in 1923 and was buried near her husband in the Suquamish Cemetery.

BIHS 38

Chapter Three

The Explorers

The serenity of the climate, the innumerable pleasing land-scapes, and the abundant fertility that unassisted nature puts forth, require only to be enriched by the industry of men with villages, mansions, cottages and other buildings, to render it the most lovely country that can be imagined . . .

—George Vancouver, May 18, 1792

He was late and in a hurry. He had missed the Columbia River. And negotiations had stalled with the Spanish over who should control the Northwest coast.

Things were not going well for George Vancouver, captain of His Majesty's surveying ship HMS *Discovery* as he spent his first night in the strait named for Portuguese adventurer Juan de Fuca. At dawn, Vancouver gave orders to his crew to weigh anchor and take advantage of the light northwesterly breeze that would carry them into the uncharted channel ahead. Snow-clad Mount Olympus lay to the southwest, and more snowy peaks rose to the east dead ahead.

The breeze ruffled the cobalt waters between the mainland and several islands to the north. He made note of the points of reference provided by enormous snow-clad volcanoes to the north and southeast as his stubby ship felt its way south, crew members in the forechains probing for shoals.

Murray Morgan, author of *Puget's Sound,* tells the story:

Late on the sunny afternoon of Saturday, May 19, 1792, His Britannic Majesty's sloop-of-war *Discovery* dropped anchor in 210 feet

Opposite: *HMS* Discovery, *right, prepares to drop anchor off Bainbridge Island's Restoration Point near HMS* Chatham *in this carefully researched pencil drawing by Bellevue maritime artist Hewitt Jackson.*

Courtesy of Hewitt Jackson
and Jim and Mary Dahlquist

of water over sandy bottom in mid-channel between Blake and Bainbridge islands three miles west of Alki Point. Three hundred years after the European discovery of America, white men had reached the area of Tacoma and Seattle.

From the deck of the three-year-old ship, George Vancouver studied his surroundings. He was a dour man of Dutch descent, little given to poetic expression, but he was moved by the splendor of the sea in the forest, which he was the first to describe. The waterway lay cradled between mountain ranges. To the east, the Cascades "in various rugged and grotesque shapes rear their heads above the lofty pine trees that appear to compose one uninterrupted forest between us and the snow range." To the west lay "the ridge of mountains on which Mount Olympus is situated, whose rugged summits are seen no less fancifully towering over the forest."

The land nearest the *Discovery* was a finger of sandstone pointing eastward, its surface "a beautiful meadow covered with luxuriant herbage." Indian women were digging bulbs with fire-hardened sticks. At the far edge of the meadow, against the dark forest, dimly seen from the ship, were scattered make-shift shelters formed by covering a loose frame of poles with rush mats.

This was a summer encampment. The Indians—Suquamish—had come to gather food. They paid remarkably little attention to the *Discovery,* the first ship to visit their area. Although several canoes were drawn up on the rocky beach below a low bluff, only one was launched. Two naked men paddled the blunt-nosed dugout as it circled the hundred-foot-long, copper-sheathed warship, slowly and at a most respectful distance. For a long time the paddlers ignored the calls of greeting, the beckoning gestures, and the displays of trinkets.

Murray doesn't point out one important factor affecting Vancouver on this first visit of a European to the body of water he named for his second lieutenant, Peter Puget. He was more than a month behind schedule. His voyage had begun thirteen months before in Portsmouth, England. Thirty-four is young for a ship's captain charged with the enormous task of charting huge tracts of the Pacific Ocean and the coastline of the entire North American continent. But Vancouver already had been at sea for more than twenty years. He was the product of Captain James Cook's rigorous training. Cook's influence also explains why Vancouver chose to use the same kind of ship, a stout, 340-ton Whitbey collier—coal carrier—that Cook had used.

Discovery had a crew of one hundred. Vancouver also was assigned a smaller armed tender, the 135-ton *Chatham*, with a complement of forty-five men commanded by Lieutenant William Broughton. They had sailed on All Fools Day, 1791, from Falmouth Harbor.

Vancouver's official orders were to proceed to Nootka Sound on the west coast of Vancouver Island to receive back from the Spanish government "the buildings and tracts of land, situated on the north-west coast above mentioned, or on islands adjacent thereto, of which the subjects of his Britannic Majesty were dispossessed about the month of April, 1789, by a Spanish officer."

But his secret orders were to continue Cook's work in charting the West Coast from California to Alaska, trying to identify waterways that might lead to an easier route to the Great Lakes.

It took Vancouver's two ships a year to get to Hawaii. They spent three weeks taking on supplies and set sail for the coast March 18, 1792. A month later, they were surveying the California coast.

In a hurried week at the end of May, Vancouver and his crew charted Puget Sound from Discovery Bay to present-day Olympia. Lying at anchor off the southern tip of Bainbridge Island that first evening of May 19, Vancouver wrote out orders for Lieutenant Peter Puget to leave at four o'clock the next morning in the *Discovery's* twenty-foot launch, accompanied by Joseph Whidbey in the cutter, to go through Colvos Passage between Vashon Island and the Kitsap Peninsula to determine the extent of the waterways south of them.

Meanwhile, Vancouver's men took advantage of Blakely Harbor to find replacements for several broken spars that supported the topsail on the foremast, which had given way as the *Discovery* neared Point No Point. Vancouver appreciated the wealth of timber around him.

Spruce Beer

Captain James Cook's favorite recipe, believed to have been used by Captain George Vancouver's men:

To 6 gallons of water add 3 1/2 pounds of outer sprigs of spruce branches and boil for six hours. Strain.
Add 7 pounds of molasses, boil.
Add 4 tablespoons dried yeast, allow to ferment.
Add small amount of rum or arrack and brown sugar. Stir.

- Hewitt Jackson

". . . [A]nd it was a very fortunate circumstance, that these defects were discovered in a country abounding with materials to which we could resort; having to make our choice from amongst thousands of the finest spars the world produces," he wrote. "Some beer was brewed from the spruce, which was here very excellent, and the rest of the crew were employed in a variety of other essential services."

From his anchorage, Vancouver could see three of Washington's volcanoes.

"To describe the beauties of this region, will, on some future occasion, be a very grateful task to the pen of a skillful panegyrist," he wrote in his diary. "The serenity of the climate, the innumerable pleasing landscapes, and the abundant fertility that unassisted nature puts forth, require only to be enriched by the industry of man with villages, mansions, cottages, and other buildings, to render it the most lovely country that can be imagined; whilst the labour of the inhabitants would be amply rewarded, in the bounties which nature seems ready to bestow on cultivation."

With a dozen of his crew off exploring, Vancouver decided to make another attempt to befriend the natives.

Towards noon I went on shore to the village point, for the purpose of observing the latitude; on which occasion I visited the village, if it may be so dignified, as it appeared the most lowly and meanest of its kind. The best of the huts were poor and miserable, constructed something after the fashion of a soldier's tent, by two cross sticks about five feet high, connected at each end by a ridge-pole from one to the other, over some of which was thrown a course kind of mat, over others a few loose branches of trees, shrubs, or grass, none however appeared to be constructed for protecting them, either against the heat of summer or the inclemency of winter. In them were hung up to be cured by the smoke of the fire they kept constantly burning, clams, muscles, and a few other kinds of fish, seemingly intended for their winter's subsistence.

The clams perhaps were not all reserved for that purpose, as we frequently saw them strung and worn about the neck, which, as inclination directed, were eaten, two, three, or half a dozen at a time. This station did not appear to have been preferred for the purpose of fishing, as we saw few of the people so employed; nearly the whole of the inhabitants belonging to the village, which consisted of about eighty or an hundred men, women and children, were busily engaged like swine, rooting up this beautiful verdant meadow in quest of a species of wild onion, and two other roots, which in appearance and taste greatly resembled the saranne, particularly the largest; the size of the smallest did not much exceed a large pea: this Mr. Menzies considered to be a new genus.

The collecting of these roots was most likely the object which attached them to this spot; they all seemed to gather them with much avidity, and to preserve them with great care, most probably for the purpose of making the paste I have already mentioned.

The island residents were much like other native residents Vancouver had seen since entering Northwest waters. Their canoes were similar to those used by inhabitants around Nootka Sound.

Their persons were equally ill made, and as much besmeared with oil and different colored paints, particularly with red ochre, and a sort of shining chaffy mica, very ponderous, and in color much resembling black lead; they likewise possessed more ornaments, especially such as were made of copper, the article most valued and esteemed amongst them.

They seemed not wanting in offers of friendship and hospitality; as on our joining their party, we were presented with such things as they had to dispose of: and they immediately prepared a few of the roots, and some shell fish for our refreshment, which were very palatable.

Two men appeared to Vancouver as leaders of the group. One of them may have been Chief Kitsap, according to other sources, but the Englishman didn't know that. Vancouver gave presents to several residents, and the leaders indicated they would like to visit his ship.

National Portrait Gallery, London

George Vancouver

This they accordingly did in the afternoon, with no small degree of ceremony. Beside the canoes which brought these two superior people, five others attended, seemingly as an appendage to the consequence of these chiefs, who would not repair immediately on board, but agreeably to the custom of the Nootka, advanced within about two hundred yards of the ship, and there resting on their paddles a conference was held, followed by a song principally sung by one man, who at stated times was joined in chorus by several others, whilst some in each canoe kept time with the handles of their paddles, by striking them against the gunwale or side of the canoe, forming a sort of accompaniment, which tho expressed by simple notes only, was by no means destitute of an agreeable effect. This performance took place whilst they were paddling slowly round the ship, and on its being concluded, they came along side with the greatest confidence, and without fear or suspicion immediately entered into a commercial intercourse with our people. The two chiefs however required some little intreaty before they could be induced to venture on board. I again presented them with some valuables, amongst which was a garment for each of blue cloth, some copper, iron in various shapes, and such trinkets as I thought would prove most acceptable. In this respect either my judgment failed, or their passion for traffic and exchange is irresistible; for no sooner had they quitted the cabin, than, excepting the copper, they bartered away on deck nearly every article I had given them for others of infinitely less utility or real value, consisting of such things as they could best appropriate to the decoration of their persons, and other ornamental purposes, giving uniformly a decided preference to copper.

The Englishmen were a big hit. Nearly all of the residents spent the day cruising in their canoes around the ship, trading bows, arrows, garments, and sea otter skins for copper, hawk's bells, buttons, everything but what the visitors were really interested in—food. Several islanders spread the word to other tribal members, and on Tuesday, some eighty persons in two large canoes paddled out to the *Discovery*.

"They were infinitely more cleanly than our neighbors," Vancouver observed, "and their canoes were of a different form. Those of our friends at the village, exactly corresponded with the canoes at Nootka, whilst those of our new visitors were cut off square at each end; and were in shape precisely like the canoes seen to the southward of Cape Orford, though of greater length, and considerably larger."

While Peter Puget and his party were surveying Whidbey Island in the *Chatham,* Vancouver ventured out to scout the area to the west of Bainbridge Island along Rich Passage and Port Orchard Bay up to Liberty Bay. They didn't discover the narrow passage leading north into Port Madison Bay, however, and Vancouver's maps were to show Bainbridge as a peninsula. He named the point on which he had first set foot Restoration Point in honor of Restoration Day, the anniversary of reestablishment of the monarchy in England by King Charles II on May 25, 1660.

"The point near our present station, forming the north point of the bay, hitherto called the Village point, I have distinguished by the name of Restoration Point, having celebrated that memorable event, whilst at anchor under it; and from my observations made on the spot, it is situated in latitude 47 degrees 30 minutes, longitude 237 degrees 46 minutes."

He named the bay at the west end of Rich Passage for H. M. Orchard, the ship's clerk. Upon the return of Puget's party, Vancouver was done with what he called Puget's Sound. At dawn on May 30, eleven days after he had anchored off Restoration Point, Vancouver directed his crew to sail north, never to visit our shores again.

Bainbridge Island wasn't to play host to another European for another 32 years. In 1824, Englishman John Work named what we know today as Port Madison Bay, "Soquamic," according to Marriott, while he was scouting for a site for a new Hudson's Bay trading post. He chose the Nisqually delta near Olympia instead because it was closer to the overland route from the trading posts at Astoria and Fort Vancouver on the Columbia River. Native American tradition holds that several white missionaries and trappers also visited the area after

Right: Vancouver's crew meticulously charted the depths of Rich Passage, Sinclair Inlet, and Port Orchard without discovering Agate's Passage. As a result, his map shows Bainbridge Island, upper center, as a peninsula.

Vancouver. But the next extended visit didn't come until 1841 when Lieutenant Charles Wilkes led the United States Exploring Expedition to what was then still known as the Oregon Territory.

Vancouver returned to England aboard the *Discovery* October 20, 1795. He retired to Petersham, a village in Surrey south of London, where, for the next three years, he worked on his maps, charts, and the lengthy narrative of his explorations. George Vancouver died May 10, 1798, before completing them, and his brother John finished the task and presented them to King George III.

George Vancouver was buried in a small cemetery beside the Petersham Parish Church on May 18, 1798, exactly six years from the day he anchored in Discovery Bay. He was 40.

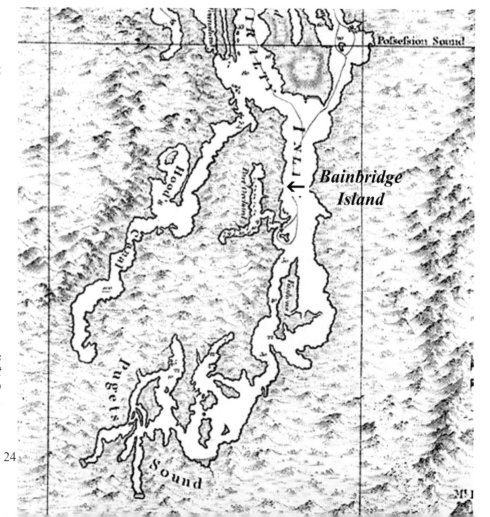

U.S.Ex.Ex.: The United States Exploring Expedition

On no account give up Puget Sound. Nothing can exceed the beauty of these waters and their safety. I venture nothing in saying there is no country in the world that possesses waters equal to these. It is the most beautiful and fertile spot in America.

Charles Wilkes, 1841

When Lieutenant Charles Wilkes and his five-ship armada sailed into Puget Sound forty-nine years after the Vancouver expedition, the area probably looked little different from what his English predecessors had seen: endless, dense forests.

Trappers, traders, and missionaries had plied these waters, but no other American ship had been in Puget Sound, "at least none the government knew about," Murray Morgan writes.

The Hudson's Bay Company had set up a thriving trading post and cattle ranch at Fort Nisqually at the bottom of Puget Sound that drew Native American trading parties from as far away as Neah Bay and across the Cascades.

The British had a steam-powered boat, and, after learning of Wilkes's arrival, its skipper generously agreed to serve as a pilot for the American expedition even though his employers knew the Wilkes party's purpose was to lay claim to the very territory the British occupied.

Wilkes spent his second night south of Admiralty Inlet in the protection of Port Madison.

If George Vancouver was the consummate sailor and explorer, Wilkes was his opposite. Here's Murray Morgan:

Charles Wilkes

Lieutenant Charles Wilkes arrived in uniform, with government ships, and he made no attempt to hide his purpose. Wilkes made a good first impression. He was forty when he took command of the United States Exploring Expedition in 1838, a tall, loose-jointed officer whose lank frame and air of dishabille were the despair of a generation of Washington tailors. An able astronomer and competent mathematician, he was one of the Navy's few scientists; though erratic in spelling, he commanded a grandiloquent prose style, occasionally effective; as a commander of men he was a disciplinarian in the beat-'em-bloody tradition of the wooden-ship navy but as demanding of himself as of his people. Wilkes's personality was his problem. He was proud, touchy, secretive; he looked on unavoidable accidents as personal affronts and on disagreement as conspiracy. Like Bligh of the *Bounty,* he should always have sailed alone. Had he been God, many a saint would have fled Heaven.

Offered scientists, Wilkes chose Navy men. When famous writer Nathaniel Hawthorne asked to go with Wilkes to record the progress of his expedition, Wilkes turned him down. The job President Martin Van Buren was handing Wilkes was every bit as important to the young United States as Vancouver's was in thwarting Spain's attempt to add the Pacific Northwest to its empire.

The British, prodded by the fur-hungry Hudson's Bay Company, wanted to claim all of the territory down to the Columbia River, where the traders had already established two prosperous trading posts. Van Buren wanted to keep the Brits above the 49th parallel. But no American ship had been in Western Washington waters, and only a few Americans had settled there. One American, who had only been as far as Astoria, called the land north of the Columbia River "extremely worthless," with "little other timber than pine and hemlock, farther inland sandy and destitute of timber."

Van Buren, who had been President Andrew Jackson's secretary of state and succeeded him as president in 1838, agreed that the government needed more information about this unknown region before giving it up to the British.

In addition to surveying the Oregon Territory and northern California, Wilkes's government wanted the world of him—literally. It ordered Wilkes to sail around the world to explore the Antarctic, to map the South and Central Pacific islands for harbors of possible use to whaling ships and merchants trading with China, and to probe the farthest reaches of the Columbia River.

The tasks would take him four years. It took him three years just to get to the Oregon coast, by which time his men were tired and near mutiny. Morale was low, and Wilkes responded by ordering increasingly harsh punishment for the slightest infraction.

"The enlisted men suffered the most," Morgan reports. "Wilkes freely applied the dozen stripes of the cat-of-nine tails, which was the maximum punishment allowed by the Navy; when that failed to achieve ungrumbling acceptance of orders, he ignored regulations and ordered twenty-four, then thirty-six, and in one instance forty-one lashes."

Wilkes reached the Washington coast in the spring of 1841. Heavy seas prevented his ships from gaining access to the Columbia River. On April 29, while heading north for Cape Flattery, he almost lost several of his ships on the Point Grenville rocks just south of present-day Tahola. Three days later, his flagship, the USS *Vincennes,* and the rest of his small fleet anchored in Discovery Bay, forty-nine years after Vancouver had taken shelter in the same harbor.

"Wilkes was unsure how the presence of the United States naval vessels, obviously sent to strengthen their country's claim in the disputed land north of the Columbia, would be received by the Hudson's Bay Company garrison at Fort Nisqually," Morgan writes. "To test the British attitude, Wilkes dispatched a message by longboat asking the help of a pilot and interpreter. After waiting a week he decided that no answer

Who was William Bainbridge?

He never sailed the Pacific Ocean. He died nearly a decade before Charles Wilkes visited the island that bears his name.

William Bainbridge's greatest mark on history was that he surrendered three of his ships to the enemy. Nevertheless, Wilkes considered Bainbridge his mentor, says Port Madison resident Edward B. Doremus in his self-published biography of the controversial commodore, *Leaves from the LOG of William Bainbridge.*

William Bainbridge

"Commodore William Bainbridge had had a colorful naval career starting at the formation of the United States Navy in 1798," Doremus writes. "Wilkes, a generation his junior, knew him well. Wilkes was appointed a midshipman in 1818 and was assigned for training to the school-ship USS *Independence* at anchor in Boston Harbor under the command of the commodore."

Bainbridge, Wilkes said, was "of full height, austere, but of a kind heart and hospitable disposition and felt great pride in the Navy and the rearing of the young officers under him.

"Very decided in his prejudices, he encouraged those of whose characters he had a high opinion but was a bitter enemy of the low and vulgar, and no officer, if he lost his good opinion, could expect to regain it," Wilkes wrote. "He could be fierce and irritable for the moment but that soon passed."

Bainbridge was promoted to first mate at age 18, and on his first voyage he helped put down a mutiny. The owners of his ship were so impressed, they made him captain of his own vessel at 19.

After joining the U.S. Navy, Bainbridge was forced to surrender his first ship to the French near Guadaloupe, the first American captain to lower his flag to an enemy. As captain of the USS *George Washington,* Bainbridge was forced by the Dey of Algiers to strike his flag and deliver tribute to a Turkish sultan. He got away with that one and received a presidential commendation for rescuing several French diplomats.

Later, while patrolling off Tripoli in the frigate USS *Philadelphia,* he again surrendered his ship after it ran aground. He and his crew spent 19 months in prison. In the War of 1812, he was promoted to commodore. Bainbridge commanded the three-deck frigate USS *Constitution,* the oldest U.S. ship still in commission, and was wounded in battle.

Bainbridge died July 28, 1833, in Philadelphia at age 59. He was buried in Christ Church Cemetery not far from the grave of Benjamin Franklin.

was answer enough and started south on his own. The next day, off Whidbey Island, a day so gusty that the *Vincennes's* lee guns sometimes went muzzle under, a dugout came alongside with William Heath, a dark-haired Englishman off the HBC supply ship *Cowlitz*. Heath piloted them to Port Orchard, where they spent the night."

Marriott says Wilkes overnighted in Port Madison. Here's what Wilkes said:

On the morning of the 8th, we made the survey of Port Lawrence [possibly Port Ludlow or Oak Bay] beginning at daylight. This being completed, I took advantage of the tide making to get under way with a fresh breeze, and passed . . . as far as a small cove on the west side of the inlet opposite to the south end of Whidbey's Island. Here we anchored before sunset, and I named it Pilot's Cove, from the circumstance of having been here joined by the first officer of the Hudson Bay Company's steamer, commanded by Captain M'Niel, who on hearing of our arrival, kindly sent him down to pilot up the ship.

We were under way soon after daylight, taking advantage of the tide, and continued beating as long as it lasted. This was about two hours, by which time we reached another small cove. This was named Apple-tree Cove, from the numbers of that tree which were in blossom along the shores. [They were actually dogwoods.] This cove answers well all the purposes of a temporary anchorage. Before the tide began to make in our favour, we had finished the survey of the cove. We again sailed, and at dark anchored under the west shore, near a fine bay; which the next day was surveyed, and named Port Madison. This is an excellent harbour, affording every possible convenience for shipping.

The scenery of this portion of Admiralty Inlet resembles strongly parts of the Hudson river, particularly those about Poughkeepsie and above that place. The distant highlands, though much more lofty, reminded us of the Kaatskills. There were but few lodges of Indians seen on our way up; and the whole line of shore has the appearance of never having been disturbed by man.

Edmond S. Meany

Port Townsend's Mysterious Poles
George Vancouver was mystified by the tall poles his expedition discovered near Port Townsend and Restoration Point, but Charles Wilkes discovered their use. The Native Americans hung nets from the poles to catch flying ducks and geese at night. This drawing, which appeared in Vancouver's journal, was done by W. Alexander from a sketch by J. Sykes.

He was moved by what he saw.

"Nothing can exceed the beauty of these waters, and their safety," he wrote, "not a shoal exists within the Straits of Juan de Fuca, Admiralty Inlet, Puget Sound, or Hood's Canal, that can in any way interrupt their navigation by a seventy-four gun ship. I venture nothing in saying, there is no country in the world that possesses waters equal to these."

On May 20, after surveying the sound, the *Porpoise* anchored in what he called "the Port Orchard of Vancouver" but sounds more like Port Blakely.

"Port Orchard is one of the most beautiful of the many fine harbours on these inland waters, and is perfectly protected from the winds," he wrote. "The only danger is a reef of rocks, which is nearly in the middle of the entrance. The sheet of water is very extensive, and is surrounded by a verdant greensward, and with its honeysuckles and roses just in bloom, resembles a well-kept lawn. The soil is superior to that of most places around the sound, and is capable of yielding almost any kind of production. The woods seemed alive with squirrels, while tracks on the shore and through the forest showed that the larger class of animals also were in the habit of frequenting them."

They spent nine days surveying Port Orchard, Sinclair and Dyes Inlets, and Liberty Bay to the north. Wilkes's crew discovered what Vancouver had not. Bainbridge was an island.

"Port Orchard [Bay] was found to communicate, on the north, with Port Madison, which we had surveyed on our way up the sound. Lieutenant Maury, with the boats, surveyed this passage, and found that it had a depth of four and a half fathoms of water at low tide," Wilkes wrote in his journal. He named the passage for his gifted artist and cartographer, Alfred T. Agate.

Wilkes named the newly discovered island for Commodore William Bainbridge, under whom Wilkes had studied as a midshipman on the school ship *Independence*. He already had named Point Jefferson, Port Madison, and Point Monroe for our third, fourth and fifth presidents. He named Blakely Rock for Captain Johnston Blakely, who had made his name in the War of 1812, and Elliott Bay after his chaplain, Captain J. L. Elliott. Sailing north, they spotted the Suquamish's Old Man House.

"Near this passage is a place where Roman Catholic missionaries have established a station for teaching the surrounding tribes," Wilkes wrote. "A large cross is erected, and a building one hundred and seventy-two feet long by seventy-two feet, which was found to contain many rude images. Many of the natives are capable of saying their prayers and telling their beads, and some were met with who could sing some Catholic hymns in their own language. The Indians frequenting this port called themselves the Je-ach-tac tribe."

On May 31, Wilkes and his party sailed north to the San Juan islands, then south to the Columbia River, their charting of Washington's ports and harbors complete.

He returned to Philadelphia in 1842 and set to work writing his report. The first five volumes and an atlas were published and present-ed to Congress in 1845, consisting of 2,600 pages and more than 300 illustrations, maps, and charts. Lea and Blanchard of Philadelphia, the publishers, only struck 250 copies.

"The whole work may be regarded as a truly national one," the publishers said. "Nothing has been used in its preparation that is not STRICTLY AMERICAN, and the design of the Author and Publishers has been to produce a book worthy of the country."

Wilkes had done such a good job that his findings were kept quasi-secret for several years to keep them out of the hands of the British and Spanish. Every member of Congress was given a copy of his report, however, leather-bound for Senators and cloth-bound for Representatives. Only 125 sets were sold to the public at the then-outrageous sum of $60 each.

Wilkes's findings had a major impact on governmental policy toward the Oregon Territory and Puget Sound. James K. Polk, who had taken office in 1845, moved immediately to acquire California from the Spanish and to settle the long-smoldering ownership issue with the British over the Oregon Territory. Wilkes's report provided the ammunition Polk's administration needed to urge Americans to settle the Pacific Northwest. That same year, the first wagon trains headed for Oregon, which was named a territory in 1848, its border set at the 49th parallel. In 1853, President Franklin Pierce split off the land north of the Columbia River, naming it Washington Territory.

After returning from his expedition, Wilkes was court-martialed on several charges brought by his crew, alleging mistreatment. All were dismissed but one, that of punishing a seaman with more than twelve lashes for stealing liquor.

Wilkes spent the years between 1844 and 1861 expanding his report on the expedition. Twenty-eight volumes were planned, but only nineteen were published. He returned to active duty in 1861 during the Civil War only to face court-martial again for intercepting a British mail boat and removing two Confederate commissioners to Europe. The act almost brought Britain into the war on the Confederate side. Congress officially thanked him, but President Abraham Lincoln disavowed the action, according to the Encyclopaedia Britannica.

Nevertheless, he was promoted to commodore in 1862 and placed in command of a squadron sent to protect commercial ships in the West Indies. In 1866, he retired with the rank of rear admiral.

He died in Washington, D.C., February 8, 1877, at age 79.

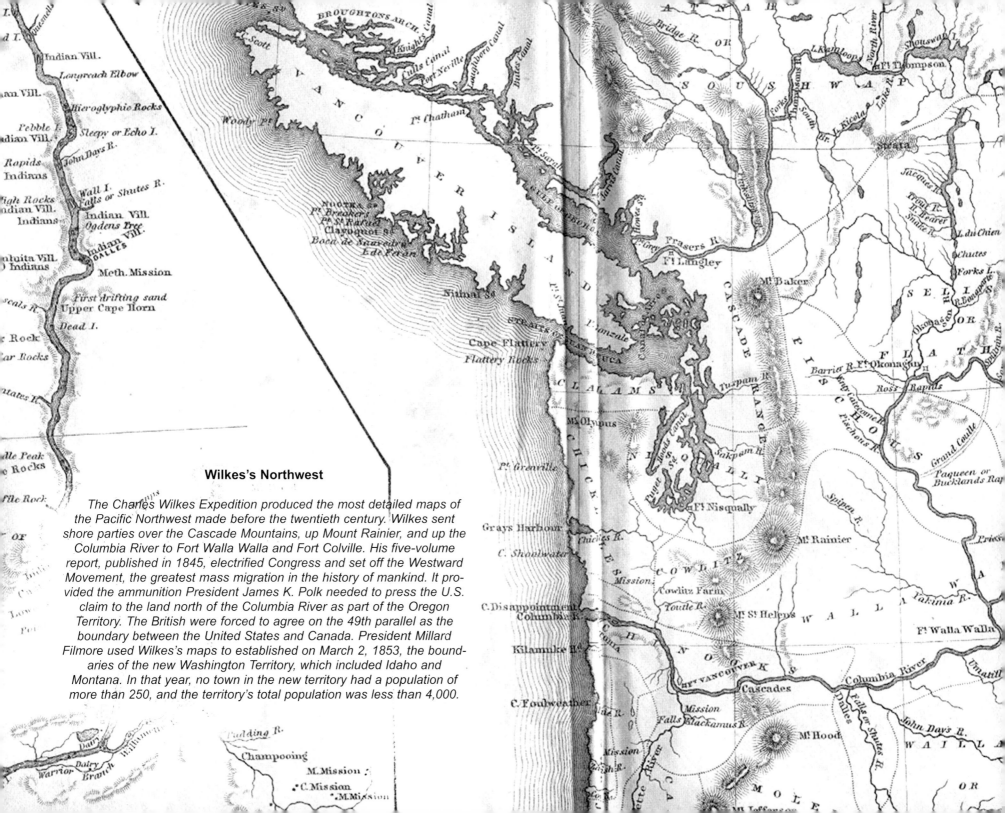

Wilkes's Northwest

The Charles Wilkes Expedition produced the most detailed maps of the Pacific Northwest made before the twentieth century. Wilkes sent shore parties over the Cascade Mountains, up Mount Rainier, and up the Columbia River to Fort Walla Walla and Fort Colville. His five-volume report, published in 1845, electrified Congress and set off the Westward Movement, the greatest mass migration in the history of mankind. It provided the ammunition President James K. Polk needed to press the U.S. claim to the land north of the Columbia River as part of the Oregon Territory. The British were forced to agree on the 49th parallel as the boundary between the United States and Canada. President Millard Filmore used Wilkes's maps to established on March 2, 1853, the boundaries of the new Washington Territory, which included Idaho and Montana. In that year, no town in the new territory had a population of more than 250, and the territory's total population was less than 4,000.

2 Warehouse
3 Court House
4 New Jail
5 Gearhart
6 Welfare
7 Allen

8 Hammond
9 Westery
10 McC
11 Ho

Port Madison c. 1861   BIHS 32

12 Sieverson-Woods (cookhouse)   21 Kiddie   —Mr. Meigs—

13 Wist   22 Boyd-Primrose-Capt. Qwindon   Compliments of

14 Bullene-Ross   23 Capt. Farnum   W.T. Worthington

15 Mills   24 Store-Warehouses-Town Hall   1878

16 Arey   25 Lombard

17 Dr. Morgan   26 Mill-Cookhouse

-Wood   X Bucklin   27 Mill Tanks

velt-Jennings   18 Beaton   28 Broadway St.

allom   19 Farnum-Morrison (store)   X Bark "Tidal Wave" (Built at Port Madison 1869)

tel   20 Mathison   ① Str. Addie (Meigs Tug)

BIHS 40

THE HARBOR
PORT MADISON, WN.
Jonnes

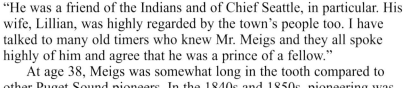

Chapter Four

Port Madison

Picture a bright, brisk April day in the spring of 1854 as George Meigs sailed south around Point No Point toward Apple Tree Cove near present-day Kingston.

Meigs was awed by the intenseness of Puget Sound. It was a land of extremes like his native Vermont, either vivid green when the sun was out or miserably gray and wet when it wasn't. Imperious Mount Rainier was "out" this April morning, its immaculate white flanks spread out above the sea of forest green below.

Meigs was about to embark on the most exciting adventure of his life. He could see his fortune packed limb to limb along the shoreline as his boat tacked against the breeze.

Meigs didn't know it, but he was destined to transform a small island nobody had ever heard of into one of the biggest economic powerhouses in Washington Territory. This new territory was empty but for the complacent native residents who showed little interest in becoming rich through trade with the newcomers. And there were precious few of those immigrants.

The handful of farmers gathered across Elliott Bay near Henry Yesler's new steam sawmill numbered about 170. Port Gamble, where William C. Talbot and Andrew J. Pope had set up their mill the previous September, was producing fifteen thousand board feet of sawn lumber, but the primitive encampment only had between two and three dozen inhabitants.

Contemporaries describe Meigs as "a fairly large man of dynamic character and a confirmed temperance advocate." He had piercing eyes and thick chin whiskers, and was blessed with a full head of hair. Katy Warner, long-time *Bainbridge Review* columnist whose grandfather worked for Meigs, describes him as "a fine man."

"He was always fair in his dealings with matters pertaining to the mill or the town," she wrote.

BIHS 1572
George Anson Meigs

"He was a friend of the Indians and of Chief Seattle, in particular. His wife, Lillian, was highly regarded by the town's people too. I have talked to many old timers who knew Mr. Meigs and they all spoke highly of him and agree that he was a prince of a fellow."

At age 38, Meigs was somewhat long in the tooth compared to other Puget Sound pioneers. In the 1840s and 1850s, pioneering was the "dot.com" revolution of its time. Its physical rigors required youth and stamina.

Pope and Talbot, scions of wealthy lumbering families in East Machias, Maine, were only 29 and 30 respectively when they arrived in San Francisco in December 1849 to make their fortunes. A company biography characterized the founders as "men of substance, experience, and mature judgment." Gold prospecting, town building, and lumbering were occupations for young men.

George Anson Meigs, born February 4, 1816, in Shelburne, Vermont, was the eighth child of Whiting and Charlotte Meigs, writes Fredi Perry in *Port Madison, Washington Territory*. George Meigs left early to seek his fortune after receiving a "common school education." He worked in Newark, Brooklyn, Key West, Memphis, and New Orleans, apparently as an able seaman. In 1849, he headed for California along with tens of thousands of other gold seekers but, like Pope and Talbot, ended up in the lumber business in San Francisco.

Selling lumber was more lucrative than mining gold. In 1849, the City by the Bay was a frontier town of shacks and unpaved streets, in a "sorry condition, streets hardly passable for mud, sidewalks only here and there, made of old barrel and hogshead staves," Talbot wrote in his journal.

Pope and Talbot had only been in town a month when it burned

Opposite: Safe Haven
By the 1920s, all of Port Madison's old mill structures were gone and the harbor provided shelter for yachts.

George Meigs, left, and Seattle Competitor Henry Yesler.

down for the second time in less than a year. Four more disastrous fires—some set by thieving outlaws to plunder whole neighborhoods—were to occur between then and June 1851. Anyone who could lay his hands on fresh lumber had no trouble finding buyers.

The problem was getting it. Forests to the north and east of San Francisco were nearly as thick with timber as those of Puget Sound, but getting the trees sawn and to market was nearly impossible with the milling and transportation technology of the day. The challenge for Meigs and others seeking to slake San Francisco's voracious appetite for lumber was the same: find a reliable supply near navigable water and a cheap way to get it to the wharves of the city.

There was no lack of competition. While Meigs and Pope and Talbot were making their plans to build mills on Puget Sound, settlers on the other side of the sound were building mills of their own. Big Mike Simmons, member of the first wagon train to reach Puget Sound in 1845, had built a water-powered sawmill in Tumwater in 1847. The output was so small, and demand so great, that Simmons couldn't produce enough to sell elsewhere.

In 1852, Henry Yesler began building a small steam-powered mill on the Duwamish River's tide flats at the foot of Seattle's Mill Street. The following spring, just days after Yesler began cutting boards, Isaac Parker got steam up in his sawmill at Apple Tree Cove. Parker's mill was equipped with a new-fangled circular saw blade.

But Parker had made one major miscalculation. Apple Tree Cove was too shallow to accommodate the deep-draft ships needed to carry the lumber to San Francisco. Meigs agreed to buy Parker's mill and went north to supervise moving the equipment by barge to a narrow cove south of Port Madison.

Wilkes had spent a night anchored in Port Madison, but it wasn't the one we call Port Madison today. For Wilkes, Port Madison was the whole body of water from Point Jefferson near Indianola to Point Monroe, known picturesquely as "the Sand Spit." To the explorer, Bainbridge Island's little northern bay was a "hidden cove" that appeared to be too confined for serious use as a harbor.

Meigs thought otherwise. Half a mile inside the entrance, the water was deep enough for good-sized ships even at low tide. Meigs knew that piers and pilings could supply the contact between shore and deep water that nature had not.

P.M. RAILROAD CAMP

Bess Alpaugh

Skidding Logs

The Port Madison mill chewed up logs in a hurry. George Meigs hired logging crews that built skid roads through Bainbridge Island's forests, and they dragged the logs to the mill or to the nearest body of water where the logs could be towed by tug. Two loggers, upper center, use "spring boards," anchored in notches cut into the tree, as platforms while they chop and saw the tree down. They left tall stumps because the lower portion of the tree had too much curvature for the mills to handle. Traces of the skid roads could still be found at the end of the twentieth century. It took about thirty years for the mills at Ports Madison and Blakely to clear-cut the entire island, forcing them to turn to other sources.

The *Politkofsky*

The Poly *was one of the most unusual vessels to split the waters of Puget Sound. The ungainly, top-heavy side-wheeler was built in Alaska by the Russians as a gunboat, sporting four small cannons, and was used to haul troops. When the United States bought Alaska, two Americans bought the* Poly *from a Russian prince for $4,000.*

The owners took the ship to San Francisco to replace its copper boiler, and George Meigs bought it for $22,000. Johnny Guindon, his nephew, and Alfred Welfare sailed the Poly *to Port Madison, where it towed ships and log rafts, and carried people and goods all over the Pacific Northwest. The vessel wasn't known for its craftsmanship.*

"The steamer is one of the most magnificent specimens of home-made architecture we have yet beheld," sniffed The Colonist *in Victoria, British Columbia, when the ship called there on April 2, 1868. "She looks as if she had been thrown together after dark by an Indian ship carpenter with stone tools."*

Deeply in debt, Meigs sold the ship in 1883 to William Renton for $9,000. After several years of use at Port Blakely, it was beached, only to be resurrected in 1897 to help load ships heading to Alaska for the Gold Rush. The Poly *was finally towed to Nome, Alaska, beached, and "battered to death" by the surf, Fredi Perry says. Cannons from the vessel are in the Seattle Museum of History and Industry and the Washington State Historical Society Museum in Tacoma.*

And there appeared to be enough timber within spitting distance of the mill site to keep him in business for his lifetime.

According to W. B. Bowden in his 1976 book, *Port Madison, W.T.,* Meigs and his crew of Native Americans and recruits from Parker's mill were soon producing forty thousand board feet of lumber a day, much of which went into building the new mill and shelter for his mill hands. Later on, Meigs used his lumber to build ships to haul the wood to market.

The key to profits for Puget Sound mill owners was not just having a good supply of trees, but owning the ships that took the lumber to market and having a good agent to sell it at retail. Henry Yesler over in Seattle never got big enough to do that, and he was out of business before the end of the decade.

Meigs's rapid success put Port Madison on the map and transformed the tiny inlet into a boom town, dwarfing the activities on the Duwamish. An early Port Madison resident wrote in 1855 that "Seattle is a small group of ramshackle shacks with a population of less than 150." A geography published in Boston identified Seattle as "a lumber town across the bay from Port Madison."

Meigs built wharfs along the length of the harbor north of the mill. Two businessmen named P. Hammond and H. B. Emery built a fish-rendering plant south of Meigs's mill, where they produced fish oil for the mill's lamps and skid roads. They exported pickled salmon and other fish to communities around the Pacific Rim.

The sawmill burned down during its first year of operation and then again a decade later. Meigs rebuilt larger and better plants and was able to resume production within three months both times.

Port Madison set many precedents in its early days. According to Peggy E. Drew, author of *Company Town: Port Madison, Washington, 1854-1897,* it was one of the first three communities in Washington Territory to have a circulating library. Lillian Charlotte Meigs, born to George and Mary Meigs in 1859, was the first white child born on Bainbridge Island. The home Meigs built for his family in the center of town in the early 1860s was the first house in town to have a bathtub.

Port Madison also was unusual because Meigs banned liquor from the township. Workers thirsty for spirits had to walk over to William DeShaw's trading post on Agate Point or down the east side of the island to a settlement known as La View. It was south of Fay Bainbridge State Park, apparently built on the beach above the high tide mark.

Historians are silent on the exact nature of La View, although its location is noted on several island maps, but some residents say it played a major role in Port Madison history.

Others question its very existence. According to one source, La View was a collection of beach shacks that were occupied by a tavern operator and several prostitutes who served the companionship needs of the single men who worked at the mill.

Several La View women married into respectability and helped found some of the island's most prominent families, according to the source. But La View's history remains anecdotal. A similar settlement known as Whiskey Forty also sprang up south of Port Madison during the early days but it has received only brief mention in island history books.

Meigs provided his workers and their families with "dramatic entertainments," picnics, and other diversions to keep them away from booze and other temptations. Any man showing up for work with a hangover or alcohol on his breath on a Monday morning

BIHS 1324

Kitsap County Courthouse
In 1869, George Meigs donated a lot at the north end of the town for county use.

was dismissed on the spot.

Little has been written about Meigs's personality, but he reportedly had a compassionate side that fostered loyalty among his workers. Decades after Meigs's death, a former worker recalled that anyone who came to Port Madison homeless and broke got a free meal at the company cookhouse.

Meigs built a large farm in the valley west of Rolling Bay, where he raised animals and vegetables that helped feed his workers. The farm also served as a retirement home for aging oxen that could no longer be used to pull logs, the worker said.

As Meigs expanded, so did his competition. The Pope and Talbot mill in Port Gamble had a year's head start, and the owners built a mill farther north at Port Ludlow. Another mill was under construction at Seabeck on Hood Canal. William Renton, a sea captain who had a thriving business hauling lumber, became a competitor with a small mill at Enetai across the Port Orchard Narrows from Crystal Springs before moving to Port Blakely.

Lumber prices were highly volatile. After one of San Francisco's perennial fires in 1849, common boards sold for $300 per thousand board feet, according to Pope and Talbot's official history. In 1850, the price dropped to $15 to $17 per thousand.

Three years after he had begun his new venture, Meigs managed to build the dominant industrial enterprise in the newly formed Slaughter County. Port Madison became the county seat. Meigs was one of the first county commissioners, and one of their first acts was to call an election to select a new county name. Residents chose the name Kitsap in honor of the Suquamish chief who had met Captain Vancouver sixty-five years earlier.

The first territorial census, taken in 1857, showed 169 residents in the county with 58 of those residing in Port Madison. Seabeck had 48 residents, and Port Gamble, 37. Port Orchard had 26 residents. By 1860, Port Madison's population alone was 192. The census didn't include Native Americans or the growing number of Asian workers—

Chinese, Japanese, and Filipinos—who weren't considered "residents."

Port Madison's isolation weighed heavily on some residents.

"I am so lonesome that I have a crying spell every night before I go to bed. It seems as though you been gone a year," wrote Jane Primrose to her husband Peter on June 12, 1864, while he was off in the Cariboo country of British Columbia panning gold. "Pete it's very gloomy here since the mill burned down; the machine shop, the houses on Maden Land[Maiden Lane], and one third of the houses was all burned up."

Peter Primrose, a saw filer by trade, returned from the gold fields and won election as Kitsap County treasurer. He served 20 years until the county seat was moved to Port Orchard. He also served as Port Madison's postmaster from 1872 to 1893.

By 1860, Port Madison had a machine shop, iron and brass foundry, and a blacksmith shop. A company store supplied clothing, groceries, and other goods to residents throughout the island. The mill had a cook house for the workers and a boarding house for those without families.

The county's first school, Kitsap County School District No. 2, opened in 1860 on the east side of Washington Avenue just north of Meigs Road in Port Madison. School District No. 1 was in Port Gamble, but its school opened after the one on Bainbridge. Abbie Hanford, 35, wife of mill employee Edward Hanford, 53, and mother of five children under age 13, was the school's first teacher. Her first class included at least nine other children besides her own. She was paid $50 per month.

The Hanfords' son Cornelius, then 12, went on to become Washington Territory's last Supreme Court chief justice and the new state's first federal judge. The town of Hanford near the Columbia River in eastern Washington was named for him in 1906.

Port Madison's population growth was typical of other pioneer communities.

How they stacked up

Value of Puget Sound mills in 1885

	Cut per day	Acreage	**Value
Puget Mill Co. *	300kbf	86,160	$3 million
Port Blakely	175	26,360	1 million
Seabeck	125	14,019	500,000
Port Madison	80	7,846	300,000

* Thousand board feet
** Assessed taxable value
Source: Fredi Perry, *Port Madison, Washington Territory*

Opposite: Building Them on the Beach
During the lean times when market prices for lumber were down, George Meigs had his men turn to building ships. This ship, the Puritan, *was built on the beach in front of the Port Madison Hotel in 1888.*

A Walk Near the Cemetery

BIHS 36

Mary Meigs and her daughter Lillian, left, cross a bridge built in the 1860s between Port Madison and the cemetery at the northern tip of the island. Maude, Evelyn, and Hattie Beaton pause to enjoy the view of greater Port Madison Bay. A home now occupies the site.

Families formed and multiplied, and more people hitched rides north looking for land. The new territorial legislature had held its first meeting February 27, 1854. The average age of legislators was 28, which was the same average age for Port Madison residents.

Territorial status also meant that the trees Meigs and others were cutting were no longer free. The federal Homestead Act wasn't passed by Congress until 1862, but the Oregon Donation Law of 1850 gave the University of Washington two entire townships—72 square miles, or more than 46,000 acres—of land in the Puget Sound region, including most of the unclaimed land in Kitsap County. During the pre-territorial days, loggers had just moved onto the land and claimed it, cutting trees where they were easy to get to.

In a senior thesis he wrote for a University of Washington comparative history class, Port Madison native Peter Andrew Kushner points out that what Meigs and others were doing would be considered fraud today.

"What the history of Port Madison's mill era fails to reflect is that much of Port Madison's prominence was owed to swindling and routine corruption," Kushner writes.

Meigs got himself appointed to the UW board of regents. Kushner cites one source who reported that university officials "became engaged in speculation with [UW] land holdings, the thought being that the land would yield more profit to the newly formed territory from the collecting of tax payments from private owners such as Meigs than sitting idle as university endowment property."

"Meigs was a member of the Board of Regents at the University, and had a keen interest in purchasing some of the land offered by the University, which, incidentally was referred to by Daniel Bagley as 'worthless except for timber,'" Kushner says. "By 1861, Meigs had purchased 3,300 acres at $1.25 an acre."

No matter how fast Meigs expanded his production, the competition expanded faster. New mills were popping up on every cove a boat

BIHS 2

Mary and Lillian Meigs

could reach. San Francisco, Puget Sound's best market, was boom one year and bust the next. Good workers were hard to find, and they left at the drop of a coin for better wages and living conditions elsewhere.

The years between 1857 and 1860 were financial disasters. Everyone cut production during the depression, and many of the mills' workers took off for British Columbia to pan for gold. In 1859, Yesler closed his Seattle mill. The Port Gamble mill operated at 70 percent of capacity, then stopped altogether.

Meigs and the others must have realized that their relative economic advantages— cheap timber close at hand, and easy access to deep-water sailing ships and coastal ports—were about to turn to disadvantages as a new transportation mode called railroads got up steam. Even during the best of times, Meigs's life was uncertain.

"I am damned hard-up at just this time and in fact always, but more especially now," Meigs wrote November 28, 1861, to a sea captain to whom he probably owed money. "We commenced loading the *Northern Eagle* last Monday and if I can pay her bills she will sail for San Francisco next month."

The market improved somewhat that year, just as the Civil War was beginning. The Port Gamble mill was selling more lumber, had deeper pockets, and was also buying up forest land from the University of Washington, including five thousand acres around Port Blakely for $1.50 an acre. Meigs's biggest potential competitor, Captain William Renton, was so discouraged with his mill operations on the Kitsap Peninsula at Enetai that he packed up and sailed back to San Francisco.

By 1861, Port Madison had grown to a community of fifty dwellings and shops, a school, and of course, the mill, which was capable of producing eighty thousand board feet of lumber a day. Desperate for more timber land, Meigs traded building materials worth $6,961.32 to the university for three thousand acres of land, which

BIHS 370

The Port Madison Hotel
The cause for celebration is lost, but apparently residents were overjoyed to get their view back after the big tree, right, had been trimmed. The hotel provided rooms for visiting ships' crews.

included Blake Island, 108 acres around Port Madison, and much of north-central Bainbridge Island.

It was a major gamble. The price he paid amounted to $2.32 an acre, 55 percent higher than what Pope and Talbot had paid for timber land on the south end of the island. Meigs was gambling that he could absorb the cost of producing the building materials for the university at the same time he was selling as much lumber as possible in San Francisco. The ploy buried him in more debt.

In 1863, Renton was back in Puget Sound with a partner, and they moved Renton's Enetai mill to Blakely Harbor. Renton paid $10 down for 164.5 acres at the head of the bay at $1.25 an acre. By spring of the following year, he had spent $50,000 on his new mill, and it was producing between twenty thousand and thirty thousand board feet of lumber a day.

A year later, Meigs lost one of his ships, and his mill burned down again. Mortgaging everything he had, he built a new mill with a production capacity of 125,000 board feet a day. Meigs ran from his creditors until the day he died.

Meigs's fortunes had improved somewhat in the late 1860s after he won a contract from the Central Pacific Railroad to supply lumber for snow sheds along the rail line the CP was building through the Sierra Mountains east of Sacramento. The CP was in a life-and-death battle with the Union Pacific to build the nation's first transcontinental railroad, and Puget Sound was a major source for railroad ties, telegraph poles, and bridge timbers.

After the railroad was completed in 1869, however, it created new competition for Puget

BIHS 1029

Peter Johnson Primrose
Peter Primrose had many jobs in early Kitsap County, postmaster among them. A devoted Mason, he was elected deputy grand master of the Free Masons of Washington thirteen times.

Sound mills. Loggers and mills in the Sierras had better and cheaper access to the California markets. In the 1870s, Meigs and other Puget Sound mill owners had to turn to the Northern Pacific Railroad and mining companies in Idaho and Montana.

The year 1872 is significant. Two years earlier, Meigs had won a contract to supply pilings and lumber to the Central Pacific to build bridges and wharfs in Sausalito across the bay from San Francisco. In 1872, Meigs made W. H. Gawley, his long-time San Francisco business manager, a partner in the firm. Gawley rewarded him by losing $300,000 in company funds on speculative mining stocks, then committing suicide.

The national financial panic of 1873 knocked the bottom out of the San Francisco lumber market. In 1874, Meigs turned down an offer of $500,000 for the company from the Central Pacific Railroad, probably because he had mortgaged it so heavily he couldn't deliver clear title to anything he ostensibly owned.

Meigs also faced increased competition from his neighbor at the south end of the island. In 1875, Renton built a new two-story hotel on Blakely Harbor and started daily stage coach service to Port Madison. In 1876, Meigs closed his mill for "general maintenance," and he reopened it at two-thirds capacity, lacking logs and money. The following year, Meigs reorganized the company with a capital stock of $1 million. Two years later, he sold the heavily mortgaged mill to William Sayward for $11,000, and Meigs used some of the money to install the largest circular saw in the region. Meigs kept operating the mill, but the cards were against him.

Pope and Talbot had three mills operating in Puget Sound and was top dog. Port

The Meigs Home

George and Mary Meigs built a large home in the middle of an acre in the center of Port Madison. Their house was razed along with the mill in 1909, and mill workers built a new house for Mrs. Meigs and her daughter on west Euclid. Mary Meigs died in 1919.

BIHS 48

Blakely was a distant second, and Seabeck was third. Meigs, with barely 10 percent of Pope and Talbot's operations, was last.

By the 1870s, Meigs claimed ownership of fifty-five thousand acres of timber. In 1887, a federal prosecutor brought criminal charges against Meigs for cutting timber on government land.

During the entire thirty-eight years of its existence as a mill town and shipbuilding center, Port Madison was never "out of the woods" financially. It was out of wood, literally, by 1863 when Meigs had exhausted all of the easily harvestable timber within skidding distance of his mill. He had to cut trees elsewhere and tow the logs to the mill.

"Between 1859 and 1892, Meigs and the Port Madison Mill were called as defendants in fifty-nine civil cases involving 'collection and settlement of accounts,'" Kushner writes. "Meigs mortgaged his company vessels, the *Tidal Wave, Northwest, W. H. Gawley, Coquimbo, Oakland,* and *Vidette,* four times to four different creditors between 1 October 1872 and 5 November 1878. The mortgages were not repaid."

In 1892, Meigs's debt-ridden house of cards collapsed. His largest creditor, the Dexter Horton Bank in Seattle, took title to all of the land at Port Madison and closed the mill. The Bank of England also was among his long list of creditors.

Within a year, Port Madison was a ghost town. Five years later, Meigs went to Seattle to testify in a court case, and he apparently fell off of a dock in the dark, and his body was found the next morning on the deck of the freighter *Rapid Transit.* He was 81.

That same year, Kitsap residents held an election to move the county seat elsewhere. Sydney, now called Port Orchard, got 877 votes. Chico, near Silverdale, got 43 votes, and Port Madison, 446.

In 1902, the town got national attention when an outlaw named Harry Tracy, former member of Butch Cassidy's Hole-in-the-Wall gang, made prisoners of the Johnson family for several days before escaping to the mainland. Two months later, he killed himself after being surrounded by lawmen in an Eastern Washington wheat field.

Dexter Horton died in 1904, and his successor, Norvel H. Latimer, decided to develop Port Madison as a summer retreat for the wealthy yachting set. Many of the old mill houses were moved or destroyed. Meigs's old two-story home above the waterfront, the mill, and wharf were torn down in 1909.

Latimer built an eighteen-room mansion in the middle of town where Meigs's home once stood that included a bowling alley, tennis court, and greenhouse. He named it Norvel Hall and used it as a personal residence until bank directors objected and forced him to use it as a retreat for bank employees. According to one Port Madison resident, Latimer's manse was so ostentatious that summer visitors often would walk up to his door seeking a room, mistaking it for a hotel.

Latimer enraged the few remaining Port Madison residents by expropriating the magnificent brass bell that Meigs had installed at the school, placing it at the entrance of Norvel Hall. The bell was later moved to Fay Bainbridge State Park.

In 1910, telephone service became available in Port Madison. After Latimer died in 1923, his heirs traded the unsold remainder of Port Madison to John Hudson as part payment for the Hudson Arms Apartments in Seattle. Hudson failed in efforts to market the community's waterfront and view lots, and he hired Charles Austin & Company to auction them June 4 and 5, 1927, offering easy terms with a small down payment. The auction flopped. Norvel Hall burned down in 1929. That same year, residents, who were unhappy with Hudson's oversight of the community water system, formed a nonprofit corporation and bought it from Hudson. Port Madison lost its community dock to fire September 10, 1941. Sixty years later, only shards remained of Port Madison's industrial past. Just a handful of houses on the east side of the bay dated back to the 1800s. From the west shore, a visitor could still see the rock ballast discarded by ships that came to load lumber.

The most visible monuments to Port Madison's lively past are its cemetery east of town and a small stone pillar at the juncture of the two roads that lead into the community. Port Madison's character had turned again. It became just another residential neighborhood.

Norvel Hall

In its day, Norvel Hall was one of the most ostentatious homes on the island. Built by N. H. Latimer of the Dexter Horton Bank, it had eighteen rooms, a bowling alley, tennis court, and greenhouse. Visitors often mistook it for a hotel. Bank directors forced Latimer to move his family out and let bank employees use it as a retreat.

BIHS 3083

Introduction

As the result of a real estate transaction involving the exchange of certain properties, Mr. John Hudson, well-known local contractor, has acquired title to the Port Madison property formerly owned by the Latimer Estate, consisting of some 120 choice building sites.

Mr. Hudson, not being in the suburban land development business, and being desirous of disposing of his holdings, has authorized an absolute unreserved auction sale of this property, which includes a number of waterfront lots and a number of valuable business sites along the waterfront. The auction sale will be conducted at Port Madison commencing on Saturday, June 4th, at 2:30 p. m.

Facts About Port Madison

Port Madison is undeniably one of the finest high-class summer home sections close to Seattle. Many of Seattle's wealthiest and most prominent citizens who now reside at Port Madison have chosen this beauty spot in preference to all other parts, not alone for summer use but, in many cases, for permanent homes.

Included in the lots to be sold are some of the most sightly home sites in this section, heavily wooded and commanding magnificent marine views. There are also business lots, which are bound to grow rapidly in value—there are waterfront lots, with full share rights—there are large tracts and there are camp sites—a lot to suit every pocketbook. Community Beaches provide access to the water, thereby making it possible for every owner at Port Madison to enjoy water sports at his own front door.

Buy for Pleasure and Profit

At this unreserved auction sale, which means there is no schedule of prices to be realized, the public will make the price, and that means bargains, probably the saving of several hundred dollars on every lot you buy. Your initial payment of 10% gives you possession of your lot, so you can build immediately if you wish, and occupy your own summer home this year, enjoy a dip in the briny every morning before breakfast and be at your work within fifty minutes.

This unreserved auction sale, with such liberal terms of payment, brings a Port Madison home site within the reach of most anyone, and provides an opportunity for all to participate in the profits that are bound to be made by those who buy this high-class property at auction prices.

Every Buyer will be Given an Interest in the Community Beaches

Arrangements have been made whereby every purchaser and owner of one or more lots at Port Madison will be given an interest in the ownership of the Community Beaches shown on the map herein, thereby giving to every owner at Port Madison the right to use the Community Beaches together with an interest in the ownership. The owner, Mr. John Hudson, will personally undertake to aid in the organization of a Community Club, and as soon as this Club is organized so as to be legally able to receive title, will deed to the Club for Community use the property reserved for that purpose.

Since every purchaser at Port Madison automatically becomes a part owner of the Community Beaches, every lot, no matter how far removed from the water, virtually is brought to the water's edge, making it possible for every owner at Port Madison to enjoy the delightful facilities that waterfront property affords.

FOR FURTHER INFORMATION APPLY

543-4 Dexter Horton Bldg.
SEATTLE

CHARLES S. AUSTIN CO.

REAL ESTATE AUCTIONEERS

ELiot 5667

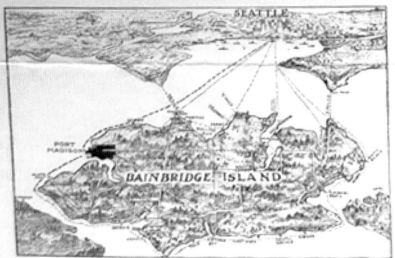

Absolute —
AUCTION SALE
of Waterfront and Marine View Homesites
at Port Madison
On Beautiful Bainbridge Island
Seattle's Summer Playground and All Year Round Beauty Spot

Stretching opposite Seattle's wonderful waterfront for a length of ten miles, with its southern extremity only three miles distant from Alki Point and its northern end an equal distance from Fort Lawton, beautiful Bainbridge Island, the summer playground of Seattle, with the majestic white-capped Olympics as a fitting background, forms one of the most charming pictures in Nature's wonderful gallery.

Port Madison, at the northerly end of this garden spot, is prominent among the delightful summer colonies established on the island. On account of its desirability and accessibility, Port Madison has been selected by many of Seattle's wealthiest and most prominent citizens for summer and permanent homes.

Commencing on Saturday, June 4th, at 2:30 p. m. the remaining unsold lots at PORT MADISON will be sold at

ABSOLUTE AUCTION SALE
to the Highest Bidder Without Reserve

For Further Information Apply

CHARLES S. AUSTIN COMPANY
Real Estate Auctioneers
543-4 Dexter Horton Building   Seattle

CHARLES S. AUSTIN CO.
REALTY AUCTIONEERS
543-4 Dexter Horton Bldg.   Seattle, Washington

46

Map of Port Madison, Showing IN RED Lots to be Sold at Absolute Auction Sa... Saturday, June 4, 2:30 P. M., and Continuing Sunday, June 5, 2:30 P. M

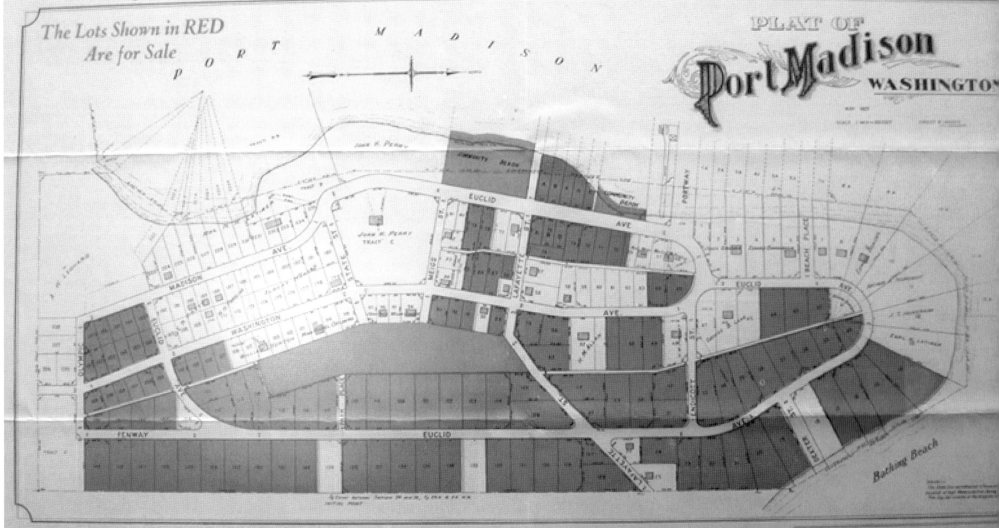

The Lots Shown in RED Are for Sale

PLAT OF Port Madison WASHINGTON

Terms of Sale in Brief

The lots to be sold are shown in red on the map herein.

Every lot put up for sale will be sold to the highest bidder without reserve.

Ten per cent of the purchase price and the Auctioneer's fee of $10 a lot required at the time of sale.

Fifteen per cent of the purchase price on or before June 20, 1927.

Seventy-five per cent of the purchase price may remain on contract, payable in installments of $10 per month at 7% interest per annum.

Lots will be sold free and clear of all incumbrances. Title insurance policies or abstractor's certificate showing clear title will be furnished free of cost to each purchaser.

The full terms of sale will be announced at the commencement of the sale, and can be obtained in advance at the office of Charles S. Austin Company, 543-4 Dexter Horton Building.

Convenient Boats

Auto Ferry leaves at foot of Mari... at 9 a. m., 11 a. m. and 1:30 p. m.

Passenger Boat leaves Pier 3, foot ...son Street, at 2 p. m., direct to Port ...

Free Trip Ticket

Present this slip at the ticket office at ...

Lots for Sale—Cheap

In 1927, Charles Austin of Seattle tried to auction off the lots formerly owned by the Dexter Horton Bank in Port Madison. The sale was a bust. Town residents formed a corporation and bought up the lots, and they also built a water system, which still is in use.

Brochure courtesy of Pete Seed

Point Agate

Looking south through Agate Passage, the unknown artist who created this painting around the end of the nineteenth century shows the bustling commerce that William DeShaw's trading post created across the water from Suquamish. He called his large store in the center of the development the "Bonanza." He named his development Point Agate. The steam tug, left, appears to be Port Madison's Politkofsky.

48

Chapter Five

Agate Point

William DeShaw strode ashore like he owned it, directing the Indians who paddled him there to unload his luggage. "It consisted in part of some leather portmanteaus, containing among other things, a sword, pistols, a bunch of Comanche scalps, a Mexican officer's uniform with shining epaulettes, and a large cotton flag which had waved above William Walker, filibusterer, lately defeated in Mexico," relates Ernest B. Bartelson in a *Seattle Times* story, *The Tragic Trader of Agate Point,* published May 29, 1949.

Filibusterer — a freelance military adventurer in search of booty — was a good description of DeShaw himself. It's pretty clear he was on the lam, looking for a quiet, out-of-the-way spot to hole up and find a new identity. The name he had been using was William Upenshaw.

What better spot than the northern tip of an island with only one industry — a sawmill run by a priggish Yankee who had banned alcohol from his settlement. DeShaw was "part of the 'Flotsam and Jetsam' that came into the sound along with the early tide of emigration," notes J.A. Costello, early historian, in his book, *The Siwash.*

"He was born in Galveston, Texas, in 1834, and at age fourteen drifted west, then north to Puget Sound," Costello writes. "He was a man of mystery when he arrived, and that's the way he went out."

"According to his own story, he had been shot full of holes, before coming to Bainbridge, while fighting the Indians," says Elsie Frankland Marriott in *BAINBRIDGE through bifocals,* "and among the trophies in his trunk, were five scalps of his own taking."

DeShaw wasn't the first white man to see the trading possiblities that Agate Point offered. J. F. and Charles Mathews had settled on the point in the early 1850s. They were fishermen by trade, however, and apparently didn't put in a lot of time building up the trading post. DeShaw knew about trading. While still in his teens, he had taken his share of the sale of a family plantation, outfitted a pack train, and had gone trading south through Mexico and Central America.

What DeShaw saw around him was opportunity. Just across Agate Passage to the west lay the thriving Suquamish Nation with its impressive timbered manse called Old Man House. Around the point to the east rose the wood smoke from George Meigs's sawmill off Port Madison Bay in Hidden Cove. On a clear day he could see the smoke from Henry Yesler's mill on the Duwamish and the growing village called Seattle.

He bought out the Mathews brothers and built a large building to house his trading post above the beach, looking west toward Suquamish. He bought whiskey by the barrel, beads by the pound, and harmonicas and pistols by the case.

He never threw away a receipt. Many survive in the archives of the Kitsap County Museum. On March 18, 1861, Plummer & Hinds in Seattle sold him ten gallons of rum for $5.56, ten gallons of whisky for $10, and fifty pounds of flour for $1.21 for a total of $16.75. When he wasn't tending his store, he was buying and selling land and logs. One bill of sale dated July 28, 1867, shows he paid William Simons $701.67 in gold coin for "two yoke of oxen and four hed of cattle including two yokes and bars and three hauling chains for hauling logs, 12 boom chains and all the buildings, houses, property and everything real and personal."

Clarence Bagley, author of *History of Washington,* says DeShaw

Kitsap County Historical Society
William DeShaw

"was among the first on the sound to make a specialty of curing herring and salmon by smoking and putting [it] up in attractive form so they found ready sale."

The business had the same ups and downs as those of his neighbor, the Port Madison Lumber Company. When Meigs couldn't pay his bills, neither could DeShaw. DeShaw once filed a federal claim against Meigs for the nonpayment of $100. Several Seattle merchants often had to send letters of demand to DeShaw.

The trader's love life was as lively as his business. Not long after his arrival, DeShaw married Mary, granddaughter of Chief Seattle. The chief often visited and stayed in a small house on DeShaw's property.

According to Bertelson, Mary bore DeShaw a daughter named Ina May, "who became one of the prettiest girls ever to grace Puget Sound." When Mary died, DeShaw married another Suquamish woman, who died after giving birth to another daughter. His third Native American wife also had a daughter. There must have been more because Marriott lists eight children born to DeShaw and his wives.

Like Meigs and other early Bainbridge Island businessmen, DeShaw was called upon to serve the newly formed Kitsap County. He was elected sheriff and acted in an unofficial capacity as an Indian subagent for the Suquamish Tribe.

Costello says DeShaw was responsible for putting the torch to their communal longhouse, which the white settlers found to be morally offensive.

"The first great duty (of) Mr. DeShaw was the breaking up of the Old-Man House and the isolation of the 600 or 800 Indians in separate households with the idea of inculcating civilized ideas of living," Marriott says, quoting Costello. "The first 'Boston' house built on the reservation is still standing (1895) and occupied by

BIHS 55

Chief Seattle's Summer House at Agate Point

one of the chief men of the village." DeShaw reportedly built it at his own expense as an example for tribal members.

As the ninteenth century ended, DeShaw's fortune was all on paper. The Port Madison mill was long closed, and the few North Bainbridge residents remaining had to eke out a living from farming or commute to Port Blakely or Seattle for work. DeShaw's customers owed him thousands of dollars he couldn't collect.

Suffering from a painful throat ailment, he stuffed his most important papers in a black valise on a cold January day and took a steamer to Seattle to see a doctor. A clerk in the hotel where DeShaw had taken a room found the 66-year-old trader on his bed, speechless and dying. His black valise had disappeared.

Transferred to a hospital, DeShaw died January 18, 1900, registered under the name William D. Shaw. Apparently because of the name mixup, his family was never notified. Two sons-in-law came to Seattle to look for the old man. They found his body at the hospital and tracked down the valise.

"It was empty and the papers that were to have saved Point Agate Store for his children had vanished," Bertelson said.

Nothing survives of William DeShaw and the Point Agate Store. A steamer dock was built westward from shore a few years after DeShaw died and the waters of Agate Passage still reveal its stumps at low tide.

A century later, expensive homes lined the shore. Tucked into a shady corner of one beach-house near the point was a small pentagonal shed with a distinctive pointed peak, apparently used by the owners as a well pumphouse.

Could this perhaps have been the cabin where Mary and her revered grandfather stayed?

There is no sign nearby saying, "Chief Seattle Slept Here."

<u>Haleets</u>

The Mysterious Ancient Picture Rock Near Agate Point

Ancient calendar? Art work of a bored beachcomber?

One of the great mysteries of Bainbridge Island is the meaning of the faces chipped into a boulder near Agate Point hundreds of years ago. Local oral tradition yields nary a clue.

John Rudolph, Bainbridge Island architect and amateur astronomer, believes the rock may have told early residents the seasons of the year.

"The petroglyph panel of faces was pecked into this polished surface at some undetermined time in the past," Rudolph said in a paper he presented at an international archaeo-astronomy conference in 1999. "The native people living in the area at the time Europeans began arriving were in awe of this stone and avoided it. When questioned as to the origin of the carvings, conflicting answers were given, but generally attributed to people in the distant past."

Native American residents apparently made no connection between the carvings or the position of the stone with keeping track of the passage of time, Rudolph said. Visiting the rock at

Ancient Calendar?

BIHS 372

No one knows who or when someone carved the petroglyph at Agate Point. These boys visited it in 1890, and A. J. Peak shot the picture.

dawn on September 21, 1997, however, he observed that the sun could be seen rising out of the deepest notch of the Cascade Mountains to the east, the Skykomish Canyon, exactly due east of the Haleets rock.

"Having witnessed the autumnal equinox sunrise from Haleets, it seemed logical that this stone with the faces pecked into the east face, perfectly aligned with the equinox sunrise, might be examined in an astronomical context," Rudolph said.

The rock, he pointed out, "has several features that are similar to features seen with the naked eye on the face of the full moon." There are seven faces in all and what is clearly a sunburst.

An observer watching the sun rise over a period of time from the rock could determine the beginning of spring and the end of summer.

"It has been thought that agricultural cultures were the only ones needing a method to determine the time of year," Rudolph noted. "Recently, it has been found that hunter-gatherer cultures needed to know where they were in time as well as in place.

"For Puget Sound tribes, the return of the salmon, the availability of natural food sources, trading rendezvous with other tribes and certain ceremonies all necessitated the keeping of a calendar. The moon could be used to note the passage of shorter periods of time, but the sun determined the year's beginning and end."

KATYDIDS

by Katy Welfare Warner

AGATE POINT, along with Agate Passage, was named for Alfred T. Agate who was an artist with the Wilkes Expedition which explored this region in 1841.

For the most part it is and has been a pleasant residential district. Its most important early settler was William DeShaw who brought this region into the limelight when he started a store which he named the "Bonanza."

Deshaw was a Texan who had drifted west with the early tide of emigration and when still a young man he came to Puget Sound and eventually to Bainbridge. He built a small house on Agate Point and a short time later he met and married Mary, granddaughter of Chief Seattle.

From his house he could look across the water and see the immense settlement at Suquamish. The activity of this Indian viallage with its braves coming and going in their conoes, the squaws busy at their tasks and the many children playing happily, possibly planted the idea that perhaps this village was a potential consumer's market. At any rate, DeShaw built his store in 1861 and it made a lot of money for him.

THE BONANZA carried just about everything necessary to a frontier establishment and some luxuries and curios as well. There were dry-goods, groceries, hardware, crockery, farm implements, loggers' supplies and even musical instruments. DeShaw carried on a lucrative trade with the natives and did a brisk liquor business on the side.

As Chief Seattle's grandson-in-law, he carried some prestige and later acted as an Indian subagent for the Port Madison Reservation which included the Suquamish Tribe. His store, which grew to be the largest in the Puget Sound area, was a fascinating place for Whites as well as Indians.

My dad, who was born and raised in Port Madison, told me that he and his playmates went there whenever they had a chance. On many occasions he and his brother, Fair, and their friends, Albert Wist and Pete Primrose, walked to the Bonanza, not to shop but just to look around, as they had no money.

Albert Wist came from a musical family and he never tired of gazing upon the shiny violin that DeShaw had for sale. While the other boys fingered the trinkets and looked at the large music box which played under a glass cover, Albert was drawn to the violin. Once Albert asked the trader if he could try the fiddle.

DeShaw took a good look at the dusty quartet and their not very clean hands and flatly refused this earnest request.

The little boy was bitterly disappointed but in later years Albert laughed about it and was able to see that DeShaw had a point. Albert was not a hot prospect as a violin buyer and the old trader was much too busy to spend time waiting for a little boy to experiment with a valuable piece of Merchandise.

A HUNDRED years later, today's merchants are still wary of small boys with dirty hands, un-accompanied by their parents, who wander through stores picking up and laying down merchandise.

DeShaw's store existed until about 1895. He was a very colorful man and was a prominent figure in North Kitsap and Bainbridge history. He and his wife had a large family and two years ago Mrs. Amy Kirkpatrick, who remembers this store, Dad and I went to Suquamish and called upon Mr. Thompson who is either a grandson or great-grandson of William DeShaw.

I suppose the location of this old store at Agate Point is now private property and not open to the public. But I wonder who is the present owners of this land which DeShaw homesteaded in 1864, and if any mementos of the Bonanza remain which would give a clue to where, exactly, it was located? It's a truly historical site.

Katy Warner, granddaughter of Port Madison ship captain Alfred Welfare, wrote a column for the Bainbridge Review *for several decades. She died January 12, 2002. This column appeared in the* Review *February 17, 1965.*

Bloedel Reserve

Stump Ranch to Forest Reserve: The Estate Known Around the World

By the time William DeShaw and George Meigs got through with Agate Point, it was a barren tract of stumps and bogs. Two lumbering families saw greater possibilities.

The first was that of Angela Collins, widow of John Collins, who had made a fortune in Seattle real estate before he died in 1903. The second was that of Virginia and Prentice Bloedel, who in 1951 bought the house that Angela Collins built.

When Washington became a territory in 1853, land on northern Bainbridge Island was held in trust for the Territorial University, according to Lawrence Kreisman, author of *The Bloedel Reserve: Gardens in the Forest*. In 1862, Meigs paid the university $4,000 for 2,675 acres of land on the point. Meigs's mill cut timber from the property into lumber that was used to build the university's first building, Kreisman says.

In 1904, Angela Collins bought forty-five acres near the point for a summer retreat. She and her children built a one-room cabin on the beach, but she yearned for a permanent residence in the style of a French villa. It was completed in 1932, and Mrs. Collins divided her time between it and her Seattle mansion. The Bloedels bought it in 1951, enlarged the estate, and created a treasure house of gardens and forests that has attracted visitors to the island from around the world.

Upper right: *Charcoal sketch shows the architect's original idea for Angela Collins's new home, completed in 1932.*
Bloedel Reserve

Lower right: *After they bought the property in 1951, Virginia and Prentice Bloedel turned the grounds into a wonderland of Northwest flora and scenic trails.*
Mary Randlett

Near right: *Promotional brochure published in 1950 extolls the virtues of the Collins property, which had stood vacant several years.*
Bloedel Reserve

Magnificent Pacific N.W. Home for Sale

Settlement of an estate now makes available one of the fine residential properties of the Puget Sound area. "Collinswood" is a charming, 15-room modern home on Bainbridge Island, 8 miles from the City of Seattle.

Collinswood stands on a beautifully landscaped knoll overlooking Puget Sound, with the Cascade Mountains in the background. A private, fine sandy beach fronts the property on the salt waters of the Sound.

This is an exceptional opportunity to buy reasonably a lovely, spacious family home in a setting of striking beauty—a green wonderland of scenic pleasure the year around. Here is restful quiet with every convenience and recreational facility of modern living.

Seabold: Norwegian Enclave

Seabold School, right, was the center of a Norwegian farming community west of Port Madison in the 1880s. John and Anna Johnson, whose home is on the left, donated the land for the school, and the Port Madison mill provided the lumber after eighteen families petitioned the county to recognize the newly formed District 28. The school closed in 1928. The Seabold Community Club purchased the building for community and cultural activities.

BIHS 1053

Chapter Six

Seabold/Manzanita

When William Bull and John Johnson started a community in the northwest corner of Bainbridge Island around 1880, the area soon got a name nobody wanted.

"The place was first called 'Bull Town,'" writes Elsie Frankland Marriott in *BAINBRIDGE through bifocals.* "From that time on there was a gradual settling of the locality—mostly shipworkers. Mr. Johnson and Mr. Bull sub-divided their homesteads and sold property to the settlers, many of whom still live on their original tracts.

"Mr. Nelson built a store and postoffice where the North Seabold dock was later located. The name 'Seabold' was decided upon when the postoffice was established in 1892, because of the proximity of the place to a tidal shore. Nils P. Nilson was the first postmaster, and 'Old Tom' (Solomon E. Thomas) fetched the mail from Port Madison by rowboat, and then carried it to the postoffice on foot."

Bill Bull didn't object to the name change, says Katy Warner in *A History of Bainbridge Island.*

"Mr. Bull wanted to make a big town out of Seabold. Before long everyone was calling this place Bull's Town," she wrote. "Even Mr. Bull did not think that this was a very good name. He set out to change it. When Mr. Bull arrived in Seabold from Norway, it was a windy, stormy day. The waves were hitting the beach and he thought, 'The sea is bold today.' Sometime later he thought of that day and named the place Seabold."

Seabold residents built their own school.

"The children at first walked or went by rowboat to Port Madison to school," Marriott says. "Then for a time classes were held in a small house opposite the present location of the Church. Then in 1894, Mr. Johnson donated land and a school house was built. Mr. Bull donated land for the cemetery. The Church was organized in 1908."

Amanda Johnson succeeded Nilson at the post office and was Seabold's postmistress for thirty-eight years.

Seabold had two steamer landings in the early 1900s. When the island's school districts consolidated in 1928, Seabold residents took up a collection and bought the school for use as a community hall. Seventy-five years later, it was still in active use.

Bull also homesteaded on the bay south of Seabold. That bay was surrounded by magnificent red-barked madrona trees. But the bay was misnamed for a tree that grows in the Southwest deserts.

"Manzanita Bay was first called 'Mosquito Bay,'" Marriott says. "When the post office was established in 1900, the name 'Manzanita' was adopted by Mrs. Wheeler, the first postmistress, because of the belief that the Madrona trees were Manzanita trees."

Orme Selland, who had operated a store in Seabold, moved a mile south to Manzanita Bay in 1895. The store and post office were built on a dock on the bay's northern point. The Seattle Yacht Club "extended its activities" to the bay in 1908, Marriott says. The store and post office closed in 1927, and the dock was torn down.

"The 'Great American Blue Fox Farm' owned and operated by Z. Peck, and S. V. B. Miller, was located on Manzanita Bay about 1924, and was the largest pen-raised Blue Fox Farm in the Pacific Northwest," Marriott writes, "there being some 68 breeding pens and over 130 Blue Foxes, representing an investment of [about] $50,000."

That spot has a magnificent view of the Olympic Mountains, and it attracted several families of national prominence.

"In 1930, after the Lindbergh and other kidnapping tragedies in the East, Mr. and Mrs. George Westinghouse Jr., parents of two young sons, sought the seclusion of Bainbridge shores, and built an impressive and costly residence which, now abandoned, stares blindly into the east arm of Manzanita Bay," Marriott wrote in 1940.

Marriott was wrong about the date of the Lindbergh kidnapping.

In 1965, Jon and Barbara Robbins Lindbergh bought the former Westinghouse mansion at the head of what was called Little Manzanita Bay and raised five children in it over the next twenty years. Jon was the oldest surviving son of Charles and Anne Morrow Lindbergh. Jon's older brother, Charles Jr., was kidnapped in March 1932 while his mother was pregnant with Jon.

The Silvens Make Hay

John Silven married one of pioneer resident John Johnson's daughters and homesteaded some of the best farmland on the north end of the island. Eventually, Norwegians held all of the land between Port Madison Bay and the western water's edge.

Several communities grew up near Manzanita Bay's southern inlet, including Arrow Point, Venice, Battle Point, and Tolo. Venice Landing, on the west side of the peninsula that protects Manzanita Bay, had a wharf 780 feet long, the longest in Puget Sound waters when it was built in 1908, according to Marriott. Venice was one of eleven stops that steamers made on the two-hour trip between Poulsbo and Seattle.

Venice was also home for a famous tree.

"At Venice, today, (named after Venice, California) an old skid road—reminder of the logging days—leads down into a swale," Marriott says. "There stands 'Bill Taft,' the largest living Douglas fir on Puget Sound, which was left standing because it was too large to handle. Its circumference is thirty feet, and it reaches two hundred feet into the sky. For 700 years or more this grand old giant has stood to sentinel the Sound."

Seattle clergymen often came to the island to hold open-air church services near the base of the mighty tree, Marriott says.

Arrow Point got its name from the many Native American artifacts found on the point, "some deeply imbedded in the earth," she writes.

Battle Point "was named because of a battle which was fought there at an early time, between the local Indians and the northern Indians, in which Chief Kitsap and his men were victorious."

The Dock at Manzanita

For the first thirty years of the twentieth century, the dock on Manzanita Bay was a thriving point of commerce. Farmers shipping goods by steamer stored them in the warehouse at right. The post office and general store were at the shoreside end of the pier with living quarters above. Oral tradition claims that, during the prohibition era, the dock served as a night-time off-loading point for Canadian whiskey. The house, far left, reportedly began as a barn and was later converted to a house. No sign of the dock and store remains. But the house across what is now Manzanita Road survives into the twenty-first century. The public road end that served the dock has become a summer gathering place for neighborhood residents and boating enthusiasts.

The "Largest Mill in the World"

This and the photos on the two preceding pages make up a panorama of Blakely Harbor's north shore with the second of its three mills around the turn of the twentieth century. The mill could produce 500,000 board feet of lumber a day and was known as the world's largest lumber mill. In 1907, the mill was heavily damaged by fire and, when rebuilt, only had a capacity of 300,000 board feet per day. The Hall Brothers' shipyard is in left center.

Chapter Seven

Port Blakely

The company that Captain William Renton built is one of the great success stories of the Pacific Northwest. Its economic power in the late nineteenth century helped propel Washington Territory to statehood. Even into the twenty-first century, Port Blakely Mill Company and its corporate relatives continued to create wealth from the region's forests.

But Renton almost blew it. Despite his skill as a sea captain in keeping his vessels off rocky shoals, he was a lousy judge of mill sites. It took him more than 10 years to find a safe harbor for his mill when it was never more than four and a half miles away. By then, he was close to bankruptcy and ready to give up. But let's start at the beginning.

"In 1852, just before his thirty-fourth birthday, Renton made his first trip to Puget Sound," writes Andrew Price Jr. in his definitive history, *Port Blakely, the Community Captain Renton Built.* "He captained the bark *Alabama*

BIHS 1196
William Renton

on a voyage north and up the sound to Steilacoom in Washington Territory. He returned to San Francisco with a load of piling, leaving Steilacoom on October 26 and reaching San Francisco Bay on November 7. He liked what he saw on the sound and recognized that a great opportunity awaited the person who could put together the capital for a sawmill, locate and manage the mill properly and have a part-

ner in San Francisco to market its products." Renton made it to the sound ahead of George Meigs, but J. J. Felt was already at Apple Tree Cove with the same idea. Henry Yesler had just gotten his new mill going over on the tideflats of the Duwamish River. Andrew Pope and William Talbot, whom Renton probably had met in San Francisco, were looking at sites at Port Ludlow and Port Gamble.

Renton had good reasons for seeking a more stable and prosperous life ashore, and he had good credentials for entering the lumber business. Born November 2, 1818, in Nova Scotia, he was brought up in a lumbering and ship-building community, Price reports. His father, a sailor, died when William was eleven, leaving the boy to support his mother and three sisters. At eighteen, he was an officer aboard a U.S. merchant ship, and, when he was twenty-three, he became a U.S. citizen.

About the same time, Renton married his recently

BIHS 1199
Sarah Renton

widowed landlady, whose husband, a ship captain, had died at sea. Sarah brought to the marriage her house, $2,000 in savings and cash, and three young daughters.

Using his wife's money, Renton began buying and selling ships. The family ended up in San Francisco in 1850, during the frenzy of the California gold rush. Renton wisely chose to deal in lumber from a beached sailing ship rather than chase after gold.

After his 1852 trip to Puget Sound, Renton found backers to help finance equipment for a mill. Renton sailed right past Bainbridge Island's three well-protected harbors and fell under the spell of Seattle land speculator Charles C. Terry. Price describes the result:

> Terry had just begun to promote the development of a village at Alki Point, in present-day West Seattle, and he persuaded Renton to place his mill there. . . . Writing in 1905 of his first visit at Alki in early June of 1853, pioneer Ezra Meeker recalled, "Captain Renton had built some sort of a sawmill here, that laid the foundation to his great fortune accumulated later at Port Blakely."
>
> Renton ran into problems as soon as his mill began producing boards. In 1888, pioneer A. A. Denny wrote, "It now seems strange that men of such marked intelligence and experience as they (Captain Renton and J. J. Felt) possessed could have overlooked and passed by such superior locations as Madison and Blakely. I suppose it was on the theory that Puget Sound is all a harbor, and it was not necessary to be particular."
>
> Captain Renton learned that he should have been particular, that Alki Point was exposed to winds from the north as well as the south, that vessels could be blown ashore and logs blown away and that he had chosen a very poor site for his mill.

Renton lost his California partners. In 1854, he and a new partner, Daniel S. Howard, moved Renton's machinery to what is now Enetai on the Port Orchard Narrows across from Bainbridge Island's Crystal Springs. Another bad choice.

The mill site was on the west side of the waterway and somewhat more protected than Alki, but sailing ships had great difficulty getting to it because of the capricious winds in Rich Passage and the narrows.

Speaking years later about getting to the mill in the 1860s, Captain W. B. Seymore recalled, "We then made sail again from Seattle, so unimportant a town that no one cared to go ashore, crossed the sound and worked our way up through Port Orchard Narrows, and quite a little task too, to the mill at Port Orchard, which was located about a mile north of (the future) Manette," Price reports.

Renton's Manette mill was a fair-weather operation. In winter, they shut it down and returned to San Francisco. While they were gone, a claim jumper just took over the site, mill and all. Howard's brother Edward bought him off, settled other claims, and got the mill

going again.

"I waited until they had cut a cargo of lumber, which I loaded in the bark and sent down to San Francisco," Edward Howard said. "But the detention and other expenses had been so great that I lost money by the venture."

To try to recoup some of his losses on Renton's mill, Edward Howard began farming, Price reports.

". . . [B]ought some cows, sheep and hogs; goats I had brought from Calcutta," he wrote a relative. "Started a chicken ranch, but the skunks killed the chickens and the Indian dogs killed the sheep." He and his wife deserted the place and fled back to San Francisco.

Price reports that in 1857, the mill's boiler exploded, and a heavy piece of metal struck Renton in the forehead. He suffered headaches the rest of his life and slowly went blind.

The mill lost money, and Renton and his partner had to mortgage the property. But by 1861, Renton had six white men and five Indians employed at the mill.

According to a letter the mill's engineer, David Mills, wrote to his brother, Renton had three ships sailing all of the time between the mill and San Francisco.

"But now to give you an idea of the place we live in, it is the greatest country of timber that ever was known, and bushes such that you can not walk through ten yards off the beach," Mills says.

Renton celebrated his forty-third birthday in 1861. Discouraged after operating the Enetai mill for eight years, he sold it to James M. Colman and N. H. Falk and sailed back to San Francisco to consider his future.

"Renton stayed in San Francisco for several months and recouped his energy," Price relates, "but he couldn't shake the idea of how profitable a successful mill on Puget Sound might be. In 1863, he went searching again, and near the southeast end of Bainbridge Island he found the site he'd been looking for—Blakely Harbor.

"The oft-repeated story is that he and Theodore Williams plumbed the harbor depth with a clothes line and determined that it was deep enough for ocean-going, lumber-laden sailing ships."

Reuben Bean, a farmer from Kennebec County, Maine, had been the first to file a claim January 20, 1854, on land above the harbor, which Lieutenant Charles Wilkes had named for Captain Johnston Blakely, who had died in the War of 1812. Bean's 148.5 acres

The First Mill, 1882

William Renton's first mill, completed in April 1864, was built on pilings made of green logs thrust into the tideflats. It had a capacity of between 20,000 and 30,000 board feet of lumber per day.

"reached from the south side of Blakely Harbor across to the south side of the island to what is still known as Bean's Bight and South Beach," Price says. "Like Renton, Bean may have seen the potential of the lumber industry in the Northwest."

Price speculates that because Bean and Renton shared many of the same friends, Bean undoubtedly knew of Renton's problems at Alki Point. Bean might have harbored plans of building a mill on the harbor himself, but he was killed by intruders in 1859.

"Part of his property was eventually acquired by Captain Renton's Port Blakely Mill Company, and another part became known as Ryderville, a real thorn in the side of the company that owned most everything else on the harbor," Price says.

Renton lost no time in buying up more land around the harbor. On June 30, 1863, ten years after he had gotten into the mill business, he paid $1.25 an acre for the first 160 acres on Blakely Harbor, or $200. He paid $5.63 more for an additional 4.5 acres.

"During the twelve months after Renton's first purchase of land, he bought five more parcels on higher ground, eighty acres to the south of the harbor and 160 acres to the north," Price says.

One hundred and twenty years later, the company that Renton

founded still owned more than 1,100 acres around the harbor.

Renton's new mill site was only four miles east of Enetai and just four and a half miles northwest of Alki Point, "but infinitely better suited to his purposes than either of the first two locations. It had an adequate water supply close at hand and easy to develop, and had substantially more flat ground on which a sawmill and the necessary company town could be built," Price observes. "The inner harbor would provide a good log storage and sorting area. The former locations had neither. The outer harbor was deep enough to accommodate several ships of the size needed to carry lumber to market. The surrounding hills gave protection from the north and south winds. And still the site was within three-quarters of a mile of the open sound."

Renton completed his new mill the following April. His twenty-man crew was able to cut between 20,000 and 30,000 board feet of lumber a day.

"On May 28, the *Nahumkeag,* a company ship commanded by Captain I. W. Gove, arrived and began loading the first cargo of lumber shipped from the new town that was soon named Port Blakely," Price writes. "Early lithographs and photographs of the sawmill show that it had a long ridged roof with three diamond-shaped windows at each end and more such windows on the side. Logs were stored in the water beside the mill and taken into it from the west end. There was no waste or sawdust burner; continuous chains or belts carried waste out onto open burn piles."

Price reports that Renton had planned to spend $25,000 on the new mill; he spent double that, he told his mother in a letter two years later. He also told her that his San Francisco partner had died after being thrown from a buggy, causing Renton financial problems. Price quotes the

Museum of History and Industry
Lizzie Ordway
One of the original "Mercer girls," Elizabeth Ordway came to Port Blakely from Port Madison to deal with its unruly kids. She devoted her life to teaching and was the first female elected to a Kitsap County office, superintendent of schools.

entire text of the letter.

"The parties that got the widows interest cannot manage matters, and I think we will have to separate in some way," Renton wrote. "I hope I can make him buy me out, for I am getting tired of this wooden country.

"About making money in this country: Some make, but others do not. In looking around I see that all do make that are industrious, sober and attend to there business. Liquor is the great curse of this country, as it is of every other, and it is the greatest source of trouble I have to contend with. Men are scarce, wages high and they spend there earnings recklessly. The day will come when things will be different, but it will be some time."

Renton estimated his total monthly expenses for operating the mill were about $5,000. He paid his laborers $30 to $50 per month. Mechanics made $65 to $250.

"The latter is an extreme figure," he said. "Millwrights and engineers usually get $100 to $125 per month. With board, a family can live very cheap here. No wood or water to buy and provisions cheap: Flour $8 per bbl, beef 10c, sugar 14c, tea and coffee 33 1/3c, potatoes 37 1/2c per bushel, other things in proportion. It costs 35c per man to board the men in the cook house. That is the actual cost."

Renton said he wasn't trying to encourage newcomers.

"Don't understand me that I advise any person to leave fair business to come here, and I would not advise any person to come, for the country is very wild; no schools, few churches and them poorly attended. Laws that cannot be enforced for want of good men for policemen," he wrote.

Good Neighbors

William Renton had a valuable ally in the Hall brothers, who moved their shipyard, foreground, from Port Ludlow to Blakely Harbor in 1880. Renton ran a railroad track to the shipyard to speed deliveries of lumber cut to the Halls' specifications. This picture, taken in 1882, shows the elevated walk that went up to Hall's Hill where the Halls built their houses. The brothers built seventy-seven vessels in the harbor altogether, including five steamers for use in Hawaii and forty-one four- and five-masted schooners with fore-and-aft sails that performed better with smaller crews and could be sailed without ballast

65

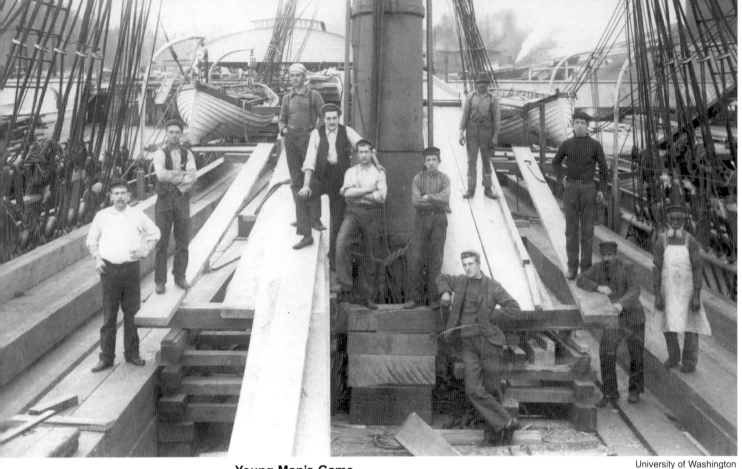

Young Man's Game
Loading a ship with boards took strong crewmen, mostly in their teens or twenties except for the cook, right. The port was often filled with ships.

University of Washington

But come they did, and soon Port Blakely had company-owned houses for families, churches, a general store, and a school. A primitive road connected Port Blakely with Port Madison and the new village on Eagle Harbor called Madrone. Boardwalks and rail lines built on pilings ringed the harbor. Renton even built a hotel.

"In 1873, a hotel, called the Bainbridge Hotel, was constructed by the mill company, and in the hotel, a saloon was incorporated," writes Elsie Frankland Marriott in *BAINBRIDGE through bifocals*. "The hotel had seventy-five rooms and a dining-room with a seating capacity of two hundred at one time. There was a broad veranda extending along the entire front of the building. Although 250 persons could be housed there, cots were often placed in the halls to take care of the overflow.

"In connection with the hotel was operated a livery barn, where single or double teams, buggies, or saddle horses, could be obtained. A cookhouse seating over 250 at one time was also part of the mill property."

Renton appears to have made money. But even in good times, he talked about selling out.

"I am in hopes to sell out this summer, when we will pay you a visit," Renton wrote his mother in April 1867. "Business is improving. When it gets good there will be no trouble in selling. About half of the mills failed in the last two years, but I think the worst is over."

"Our losses last year by failures was very heavy," he wrote later. "In fact the lumber trade is losing its attraction for me. I would rather try something else."

Four months later, he still wanted to sell.

"In a few days I leave for San Francisco in hopes of being able to sell my interest in the mill while business is good, for I do not want to pass through another two years like the two just passed," he wrote his mother in August 1867. "Every thing on this coast is overdone. You either make money very fast or lose fast. There is no such thing as a steady paying business. Everything goes by extremes. People live fast and appear never to think of the morrow.

"If I can sell out, Martha and I will pay you a visit." (Renton often called his wife Martha rather than Sarah.)

Less than a year later, he reported that his partners couldn't buy him out because the business was worth too much money. The mill

66

Sea of Masts

The first mill can be seen in the background as ships crowd the loading dock in 1882.

was running around the clock, cutting an average of 70,000 board feet a day. Renton reported that the company shipped five million board feet of lumber during the first four months of 1868. Five ships were in port loading lumber, three of which were owned by Port Blakely.

"We go on the principal[sic] 'make hay while the sun shines,'" he wrote.

Despite his constant pessimism, Renton was clearly a good businessman, a cut above his competitor on the north end of the island. In the final years of the 1860s, both were taking advantage of the huge demand for lumber created by San Francisco's tremendous growth and construction of the transcontinental railroad.

Alongside the railroad, crews were building a telegraph line that would stretch unbroken from San Francisco to the East Coast. George Meigs won a Central Pacific contract to supply boards for snow sheds to protect its line from the heavy snows of the Sierras. To keep up, Renton's mill began making what companies today call "value-added products." Renton and his managers were pioneers in the field with prefabricated windows, doors, and porch panels for houses. Houses all over the island still have windows with frames stamped, *Port Blakely Mill Co.*

For Northwest lumber barons, the 1860s and 1870s were among the most volatile periods in history. Steam power made them and then broke them. They built railroad tracks through virgin forests so they could use steam "donkeys" equipped with drums of cable to haul logs out of the forests to railroad cars that carried the logs to tidewater dumps. Steam-powered tugs towed log rafts—called "booms"—to the mills where steam engines created power for their saws and conveyor

67

A Company Town . . .
Standing at the foot of the boardwalk that went up Hall's Hill in 1882, Carleton Watkins
photographed Port Blakely's first mill and company houses. His darkroom tent is in the foreground.
The houses had no two-by-four studs. Heavy siding provided the rigidity.

. . . and How It Grew

Port Blakely was a busy place by the turn of the century with the second mill in full production. Houses sported porches and decorative picket fences with mill work done in a special shop. The white building at the end of the houses, center, is the Bainbridge Hotel.

69

belts.

Their competitors on the mainland were doing the same thing. Mills multiplied as the railroads pushed farther inland. But Port Blakely's biggest competition was closer to home. In 1858, Pope and Talbot had the largest enterprise in the territory and it remained so for the rest of the nineteenth century. It was better financed, but, like the mills on Bainbridge, was dependent on ships for transporting lumber to market.

By 1879, the three mills owned by Pope and Talbot's Puget Mill Company in Port Gamble, Port Ludlow, and Utsalady up on Camano Island had a combined output of 235,000 board feet a day, almost twice as much as the combined output of Port Madison and Port Blakely. In 1881, according to Marriott, the Port Blakely Mill Company's capital stock was worth $500,000 and the company owned more than 80,000 acres of timber land.

In 1882, Renton bought 22,000 acres of timber in Mason County, and the company's holdings eventually grew to more than 100,000 acres. Price reports Renton also got into the coal business and helped finance a railroad from Seattle to Walla Walla, but it never got beyond Maple Valley southeast of Seattle.

During the 1880s, the Bainbridge Island mills made Kitsap County an economic powerhouse that helped propel Washington to statehood in 1889.

"The two mills on Bainbridge Island, together with three others on the mainland, promoted Kitsap County to first place industrially of all the counties in the state," Marriott wrote. "In fact, not only was it for a quarter of a century, by three times the most industrial county of the state, but in proportion to population, it was the richest county in the country."

By the end of the 1880s, there were 310 sawmills operating in Washington. Fifteen years later, there were nearly one thousand.

The competition had begun taking its toll five years earlier. In 1884, Puget Mill Co. closed its mills in Port Ludlow and Utsalady. Its Port Gamble mill was operating at fifty percent of capacity. The following year, Port Madison had only seventy men working three-quarters time.

In 1886, the Dexter Horton Bank began threatening foreclosure on Meigs's loans for the mill at Port Madison. Workers at Port Blakely struck, demanding reduction to a ten-hour work day. Renton paid the

BIHS 2181

All Dressed Up
Wedding? A Port Blakely family was celebrating something special.

workers off and closed the mill. Port Madison doubled its output to capitalize on the closure, forcing Renton to reopen his mill.

On February 4, 1888, the Port Blakely mill burned to the ground at an estimated loss of $250,000. In a feat of financial and technological wizardry, Renton got the wood-cutting machinery back in operation within sixty days and rebuilt the mill in "exactly five months to a day from the time the fire started," according to Marriott.

The new mill's output was 300,000 board feet per day. At the time, Port Blakely's population was estimated at one thousand persons.

On June 5 the following year, Seattle's eighty-acre downtown burned down. The city's population was forty thousand. Local mills saw some increase in business from rebuilding Seattle, but city fathers wisely chose to use brick and stone for most of their new buildings.

Captain Renton's new mill was a marvel of efficiency for its day. Compared to today's mills, however, it produced a lot of waste in the form of sawdust, useless slabs, and heavy smoke.

"The mill had its own planing mill, sash and door factory and dry kiln," Marriott writes. "It also had its own generating plant and furnished electricity for the mill and the town. There were two chemical tanks and a hose cart for fire protection. A complete system of automatic water works was built throughout the entire mill plant.

"A high iron Trestle carried off the slabs to an enormous fire which never ceased to burn, and where all the waste was consumed. In this connection we might add that the waste was tremendous. The six-foot circular saws of the early days cut a kerf one-half inch wide, and as a result a great deal of the log was wasted—the question being not how to utilize the slabs, sawdust and other refuse, but how to get rid of it. Therefore it was all burned in those unquenchable fires."

The mill became known as "the largest sawmill in the world" and in 1890 was responsible for shipping almost a quarter of the lumber produced on Puget Sound, Price says.

"That year, 105 heavily loaded lumber ships left its docks," he writes. "When the figures for other mills on the sound were gathered, it was determined that the entire Puget Sound lumber fleet shipped a total of 430 cargoes. The thrill was that nearly a quarter of them had left from Port Blakely and that the next largest shipper was the Port of Tacoma, which reported the departures of 71 ship loads of lumber that year."

But the 1890s saw the end of the Rentons. Sarah Renton died May 12, 1890, at Port Blakely and was buried in Lakeview Cemetery on Seattle's Capitol Hill. She was 74.

A year later on July 18, 1891, Captain Renton, 72 and blind but still actively running his company, "died of peritonitis at his sister's home," Price reports. "His illness was a short one. True to form, he is said to have been in consultation about mill business on the day of his death."

The mill closed for three days. George Meigs of Port Madison, Henry Hall and his son James of the Hall Brothers Shipyard, and the greats of Seattle's business community came to mourn

BIHS 2212

Cozy Kitchen
Mill house kitchens were spartan. The calendar on the wall is for August 1892.

Second Mill Under Construction

Fire, the fear of every mill owner, destroyed Port Blakely's first mill February 4, 1888. Renton had its saws cutting boards again in sixty days and completed a new building in five months. It cut 300,000 board feet per day, and later, 500,000.

him. More than a thousand mourners filled the Port Blakely home of his sister, Mary Renton Campbell, where his body lay in the front room in a black casket with silver side-bars.

Pall bearers wrestled the heavy man and his coffin onto the *Politkofsky* at low tide, and a flotilla of seven boats accompanied the captain to Seattle where another service was held. And "135 carriages, cabs and buggies" accompanied his casket to the cemetery on Capitol Hill, Price says.

Sarah Renton's daughters put up a brief legal fight for Renton's $3 million estate, which he had left to his nephews. Control and management of the mill, however, passed to nephew John A. Campbell.

President Rutherford B. Hayes visited Port Blakely in 1891. The town got good press from the reporters who accompanied the president, Price writes, quoting one of them.

Port Blakely, the site of the world renowned Port Blakely Mill, is one of the busiest and most thriving towns on the Pacific Coast, and the throb of the ponderous machinery is manifest both day and night. The noise of the whirring wheels, the heavy pulsations of the many engines and the incessant hum of the saws and the planers impress a person with the feeling that these are all a part of a gigantic living being and not mechanical devices that are controlled by human beings.

The precision of movement of the men as they work along the wharves and among the maze of ships impresses a person with the feeling that they are a part and parcel of the machinery whose throbbing is felt in all parts of the town.

Price calls the 1890s Port Blakely's "heyday years."

"One hundred and ninety-one vessels sailed from the port with a record 105 million board feet of lumber during 1895," Price says. "That was more than an 80 percent increase over the very substantial movement of 1890 that had so pleased Captain Renton. Almost as much lumber was shipped in 1896."

Fighting the railroad competition, Port Blakely built a berthing slip for barges in 1898, which was connected by rails with the planing mill and dry kiln. Finished boards could be stacked directly onto flatcars

Day at the Races

The Bainbridge Hotel was a community gathering place, attracting many activities, including this velocipede race. The hotel featured a thirty-foot-long porch, a "comfortably large dining room," and a saloon. On a hot day, August 12, 1928, the hotel burned down.

Port Blakely Mercantile
With more than one thousand residents by the turn of the century, Port Blakely was the shopping center for the south end of the island.

ICE CREAM
TO DAY

The Post Office
Port Blakely's post office doubled as an ice cream parlor during the 1920s, according to Sam Whitehead of Olympia, whose mother, Nellie Klineman Wolf Whitehead, served as postmistress from 1920 to 1922.

that were towed, nine cars to a barge, across the water to Seattle's new barge terminal. Another company, Walworth and Neville, built a factory to produce telephone and telegraph crossarms with predrilled arms that carried glass insulators with lumber supplied by the mill.

At the turn of the new century, "conditions were so good that it was hard for the average person in Port Blakely to anticipate that the town might have a bleak future," Price says. But the lumber industry was still changing rapidly as bigger Midwestern companies began moving to the West Coast. One lumber baron was named Weyerhaeuser.

"Wealthy outsiders were entering the local lumber business," Price reports. "It was learned that R. L. McCormick, a millionaire lumberman from Wisconsin, was interested in acquiring the vast acreage of timberlands that the Northern Pacific Railroad had received for constructing its transcontinental line to Tacoma. Successful as the owners of the Port Blakely Mill Company were, their resources were far less than those of a number of Midwesterners."

But the railroad's timber didn't go to McCormick. It went to James J. Hill's next-door neighbor.

"In 1893 Frederick Weyerhaeuser, the quiet, industrious German-American burgher who had unobtrusively become the most formidable lumberman in the United States, bought a mansion at 266 Summit Avenue, the fashionable residential street in St. Paul," writes Murray Morgan in *Puget's Sound*. "Legend has it that when he moved in he did not know that his next door neighbor at 244 Summit was James Hill, who had just completed the Great Northern and was moving toward dominance of the Northern Pacific.

"The two empire builders hit it off. A biographer tells of

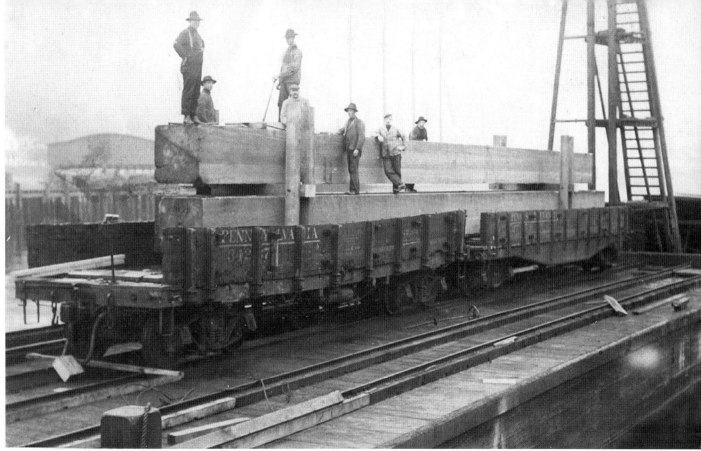

Port Blakely "Toothpicks"   BIHS 1110
The mill had a reputation for cutting bigger, longer Douglas fir beams than any other mill in the world. These beams, requiring two flatcars to hold them, are probably bound for mines in Montana. One such beam was returned to the island a century later in perfect condition.

Weyerhaeuser dozing before the fireplace in the den at Hill's place a few years later while the burly, one-eyed Canadian discoursed about the vast stands of timber in the Pacific Northwest and the low rates the Great Northern would charge for shipments east. It was hard to imagine F. W. drowsy when timber was the topic. As well as anyone, he knew that the virgin forests of the Great Lakes area, on which his fortune and his empire were based, would soon be gone."

Weyerhaeuser had considered buying timberland in the Northwest as early as 1885. Twice he passed up deals that came his way. But in 1898, he joined with several other Midwestern lumbermen to form the

75

Coast Lumber Company to take advantage of low rates the Great Northern offered in the spring when cars weren't in great demand.

"In the first week of the Twentieth Century, on January 3, 1900, to be exact, the talks that had started between Hill and Weyerhaeuser in front of the fireplace at 244 Summit reached their climax in the greatest purchase of timberland known at that time," Morgan writes.

Weyerhaeuser, backed by several other partners that included McCormick, "signed papers calling for the purchase of 900,000 acres from the NP land grant at six dollars an acre." None of the purchasers knew exactly what he was getting because the land had never been "cruised." Years later, someone estimated they had paid ten cents per thousand board feet for the usable timber.

Port Blakely's owners could see the future. With so much low-cost timber available next to railroads, those who depended on cargo ships were dead in the water. The owners let it be known that the mill was for sale. Charles Holmes, company president, was 70. John Campbell, Renton's heir, was 56 and newly married. In January 1903, Price reports, Holmes and Campbell announced they had sold their interests in the mill company to a group of investors from San Francisco and Michigan.

"The driving forces behind the buying group were David Edward Skinner and John W. Eddy, both recently of Bay City, Michigan, where their interests had been in the lumber and associated salt businesses," Price says. "Skinner was named president of the company with an office in San Francisco, and Eddy, several years younger than Skinner, became general manager in Port Blakely."

The Hall brothers needed new quarters to build larger ships, and

Mopping Up   BIHS 262
Fire took the mill's building, but the crew was able to salvage much of the machinery and equipment.

they decided to build a new yard in Eagle Harbor.

"The move had a serious negative impact on Port Blakely," Price writes. "The shipyard had employed between 50 and 100 people for 23 years. Those people traded at the store, patronized the bar and the dining room at the Bainbridge Hotel, had haircuts from Judge Plate and were brought back to good health after accidents or sicknesses by Dr. Kellam."

To keep up community morale, residents got together to build the Port Blakely Presbyterian Church. Ten years later, the Roman Catholics built St. Andrews Catholic Church on the hill overlooking the mill site.

Public spirit, however, couldn't keep the mill running. Shutdowns became more frequent. Then, another disaster. Price describes it:

At night, whatever wind there is on the harbor drops to nearly a calm. That is one of the delights of Port Blakely.

In the last days of the great mill, arriving on such an evening was special. The bow of the *Monticello* cut smoothly through the dark water, the quiet pulse of its steam engine about to be silenced for the last few hundred feet into the wharf.

Night lights were on at the MacAteer Shipyard [that replaced the Halls] and twinkling at the houses up on Hall's Hill, still called that despite the absence of the Halls. In fact, the whole north shore was lighted up, from the Williams' house nearest Blakely Point to the brightly lighted mill, where the second shift was at work.

With the conversion of the south side of the harbor to drying yards, the crossarm plant and the railroad barge slip, it was much darker there than it had been when houses were spread along it. Only at Ryderville could a little cluster of lights be seen off the port side of the entering steamer. Hardly visible were their stacks of drying lumber that stretched from close to the crossarm plant all the way to the Tsunehara's farm.

The night of April 22, 1907, was just such a quiet night. What little breeze there was, was blowing onshore from the harbor, but hardly rippling the surface. The mill company's four-masted schooner *Blakely* was tied up at the lumber-loading wharf, "stern-to," and eleven other ships were in the harbor, three of them large barks, one the British *Balmoral*.

The mill noise, seemingly muffled by the night, suggested that good times had returned to the harbor. The sounds of heavy log carriages trundling back and forth, of dozens of saws, of whistles and steam was perfect music for day-shift workers and their families to go to sleep by. Nor did the light in the sky from the huge waste burner keep the residents awake. They were all used to the bright orange glow that the burner cast on the clouds.

But at 11 p.m., tranquility turned into awesome calamity. Just as had happened eighteen years earlier, a journal box overheated, and caused a fire to start, almost explosively, in the planer room adjoining the main building of the mill. Although the mill was supposedly protected by its costly sprinkler system, supplemented by a network of fire hoses, the fire spread so quickly to all parts of the mill that the 300 men on the shift had no opportunity to use the hoses, and the sprinklers proved incapable of containing the flames.

In the absence of John Eddy, who was in Seattle, T. C. Ford, resident manager, took personal charge of the volunteer fire fighters. Hydrants and hoses were used to wet surrounding buildings, warehouses and nearby homes. After receiving a call from Port Blakely's postmaster, Harry Thomas Price, Seattle sent its fire boat, the *Snoqualmie,* to the scene of the fire. While she didn't arrive until the blaze was nearly over, the *Snoqualmie* was given credit for saving the adjoining buildings, her two-inch streams of water being far more effective than the volunteer equipment.

"The destruction of one of the largest lumber manufacturing institutions in the world took less than one hour," a reporter wrote.

The firemen saved the town, the schooner *Blakely,* and even the machine shop that was less than 100 feet from the mill.

The Last Mill

BIHS 215

Port Blakely's last mill had about 60 percent of its predecessor's capacity. It was dismantled in 1924.

"The Port Blakely Mill will be rebuilt," mill manager John Eddy announced the next day. "About 50 percent of the plant was destroyed. The loss is about $300,000 and the insurance $200,000, distributed among a number of companies. The work of clearing up the ruins will begin at once. We need all the men we can get, and I believe that all the mill crew who wish it will find plenty of work."

Squabbles with the mill company's insurance firm and a sluggish market delayed reconstruction for more than two years. The new mill was smaller with a little more than half of the capacity of the old mill. But it seldom operated at full capacity anyway.

Business picked up during World War I as the former Hall shipyard, now operated by the Skinner and Eddy Corporation, made ships for the war effort, but two years after the war ended, the shipyard was demolished. The mill closed in 1922 and was dismantled in 1924.

The only thing left standing on the site was the concrete building that had housed the 800-horsepower steam engine that turned the main shaft that provided power to the saws, planers, and other equipment.

Welcome to Pleasant Beach

Picture Pleasant Beach as a vacation paradise and weekend getaway for the frazzled business people of Seattle. This view, taken about 1915, shows the Pleasant Beach Hotel, right, and swimming pool and bathhouse on the left. Steamers called regularly at the long pier jutting into Rich Passage. By the end of the century, nothing would remain of this recreational paradise.

BIHS 1109

Chapter Eight

Pleasant Beach/Lynwood Center

Sometime around 1900, Malcolm McDonald had an idea. Why not turn some of that empty beach at the south end of the island into a resort for Port Blakely workers and their families? And that's how Pleasant Beach became Puget Sound's "Coney Island."

At the time, McDonald was manager of the Port Blakely Hotel and had built a large farming operation in Eagledale.

"He knew he would have to build his resort outside of the town," writes Katy Warner in *A History of Bainbridge Island.* "In this way, it would be apart from the mill company's influence."

McDonald thought big, but he couldn't have foreseen how popular his resort would become among off-island people. They came from all over Puget Sound, many bringing their families, to swim all day, dine in style, and drink and dance all night. The operators even staged boxing matches.

"Pleasant Beach, originally called 'Sylvan Grove,' was first settled by Asa Fowler, who entered a land claim of thirty-three acres on January 30, 1864," writes Elsie Frankland Marriott in *BAINBRIDGE through bifocals.* "This locality became very famous in that day before the automobile for its many picnic grounds and pavilions."

McDonald's wife changed the name from Sylvan Grove to Pleasant Beach, according to Warner.

McDonald wasn't the first to recognize Pleasant Beach's potential. There already was a small resort on the bay's eastern shore called "Burchillville."

"George Burchill ran a saloon, a dance hall and a three-pin bowling alley," Marriott writes. "Later, Malcolm McDonald acquired this place and put in a natatorium[salt-water swimming pool].

"Another hotel, the Pleasant Beach Hotel, was also owned by Mr. McDonald, and operated by Hugh McInnis and R. W. Huffman. This hotel of twenty rooms, in the vicinity of the present location of Fort Ward and adjacent to the beach, also had a saloon. Here, also, was a large pavilion and picnic grounds of thirty acres."

Nothing else like it existed on the sound.

"In the summer time great crowds, seeking recreation, would board the boats running to Port Orchard Bay points, and arrive from Seattle, Tacoma, and other places on the Sound," Marriott says. "In front of the hotel grew a line of majestic spreading maple trees, and a gravel roadway led from the hotel entrance to the dock where all the boats landed.

"This pavilion became famous for the prize fights, as well as the county conventions which were held there. The Kitsap County Fair began its career in this McDonald pavilion. Baseball grounds and a bicycle path attracted those who were interested in sports."

One of those fights included a World Championship match between Joe Gans and Dave Halley. (Gans held the world lightweight title from 1902 to 1908.)

Gans won, but not before several sailors, trying to get a better view of the fight, fell through the shingled roof of the pavilion into the crowded arena, according to Marriott.

Goings-on at the resort scandalized some local residents.

"Newcomers would never guess, old-timers are reluctant to recall, that this was once a district of saloons and popular resorts," she says.

The *Bainbridge Island Review* also had its office in the area in the 1930s.

McDonald invested his money all over the south end of the island, and he built a "fine home" in Eagledale near what later became McDonald Avenue, Warner reports. When McDonald built his Pleasant Beach Hotel, he "did not spare the expenses," Warner says.

"It had rooms for forty guests and its dining room served as many as 2,000 in one day," she says. "The dance pavilion was one of the best in the Northwest. A five-piece band played there throughout the summer season."

The promoter built a boardwalk between the resort and Port Blakely. But the Pleasant Beach Hotel burned down and was never rebuilt, Warner says. The resort town "disappeared."

But the resort's name did not. Over the years, land along the entire

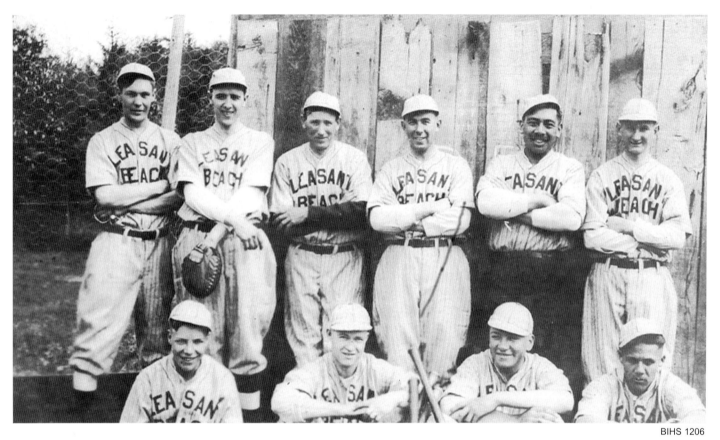

BIHS 1206

They Took Baseball Seriously

These Pleasant Beach senior leaguers look like they were something to be feared on a ball field. Communities all over the island had men's teams. This picture was taken in 1920.

"In 1936 they added the island's first real theater."

The Olsons held a naming contest for their center, and Nancy Foss won it with her entry, Lynwood Center.

Warner reports that the Olsons bought the school after it was closed in 1949 and converted it to a rest home, which they called the Bainbridge Sanitarium. It later was renamed the Serenity House. The residence next door on the hill became a restaurant.

Lynwood was a regional gathering place, particularly after the movie theater was added. It attracted residents from all over the island. The theater remained in continuous operation into the twenty-first century.

West Blakely, a residential area northeast of Pleasant Beach, had a store of its own in the early 1900s, and many of the island's most attractive homes were built there by men who were carpenters or cabinetmakers working at Port Blakely mill or Hall Brothers Shipyard.

inlet between Fort Ward and Point White came to be known as Pleasant Beach.

The former resort site became part of Fort Ward State Park.

Lynwood, just up the beach from the resort, had better luck. Emil Olson built a home on the west-facing hill above the beach there in 1898. He later sold the southern part of his lot to the county for a school, which was built in 1914. In 1926, Olson's son Emanuel and his wife Edna built a grocery store "across the road from Emil's old home," Warner says. "In the 1930s this home was remodeled in the Old English style. Mr. and Mrs. Olson added more buildings to their store and built apartments above them. They kept using this Old English style of building.

One of the best examples is the Beck House, just up the hill to the north from the grocery store and Odd Fellows Hall. The Becks became well-known regionally and nationally when in 1912 the Beck boys, along with a cousin and a dog, saddled their horses and rode to every state capital in the country. The odyssey took them two years.

After the Port Blakely mill closed, Pleasant Beach became a major agricultural center with several greenhouse complexes that provided vegetables and flowers for island residents and the Seattle market.

A Place in the Sun

The Pleasant Beach Hotel's long veranda was a popular spot on a sunny day, and its dining room and saloon were packed at night.

BIHS 454

West Blakely: A Town in the Middle

Bert and Charley Lindquist, right, bought the West Blakely Grocery from August Bloomquist in 1915, renaming it Lindquist Bros. Bert delivered groceries as far north as Island Center. Charlie had South Beach. They sold the business in 1934 to Wilbur Nystrom. West Blakely is located between Port Blakely to the east and Lynwood Center to the west.

BIHS 473

The Beck House

West Blakely had been logged off by the time that the Becks, master carpenters with high standards, undertook construction of one of the sturdiest homes on the island. It was located on the south-facing hill above the Odd Fellows Hall. Proof of its soundness was in its longevity. At the end of the twentieth century, it was operated for a time as a bed-and-breakfast inn called the Bombay House.

BIHS 3722

The Doctor's Greenhouses

Growing food and flowers commercially became a major industry on the island after the mill era ended. South-facing slopes all over the island sprouted glass greenhouses. Dr. Cecil Kellam, one of the island's first physicians, built these greenhouses above Pleasant Beach. They were managed by Seinosuke Takayoshi, whose house is at the far left. Produce from the farms was shipped throughout Puget Sound by steamer. Filipino-American and Japanese-American farmers also had greenhouses in the area. The original Pleasant Beach was on the point in right center.

Islanders of the Future

Reid Hansen

The entire student body, one hundred strong, of Pleasant Beach School turned out to have its picture taken in 1936. Many stayed on the island for most of the rest of their lives. In alphabetical order, they included Jack and Jeanette Alloin, Doris Beck, Alan Black, Amos Black, George Burke, Dick Cain, Don Dunn, Roger Flodin, Reid Hansen, Rachel Hilstad, Peggy Lundgren, Doug Nichols, Judith Peterson, James Ruttner, Sueko Terayama, Rhea Williams, and Toshiko Yukawa. The school drew children from the entire south end.

Lynwood Center in 1950

"My Blue Heaven," a musical starring Betty Grable, Dan Dailey, and Mitzi Gaynor, was playing at the Lynwood Theater in the Old English village built by Edna and Emanuel Olson in the 1920s and 1930s, starting with the grocery store next door to the theater. The center became the home of the Port Blakely Post Office, housed in the brick building, left center. After World War II, Edward "Eddie" Rollins got a job there as a clerk and was promoted several years later to superintendent, or postmaster. The Olson home, out of view up the hill to the right, became a restaurant.

Chapter Nine

Crystal Springs/Point White

The original islanders called it Tuxwaxadote, the polite translation of which is "goose droppings on rock." But Lieutenant Charles Wilkes saved us from that, naming Bainbridge Island's southwestern tip Point White in honor of James White, officer of his ship's forecastle.

The stretch of beachfront between the point and Fletcher Bay probably has had more names than any other neighborhood on the island. The area also has attracted some of the island's longest-surviving clans. Not clams. Clans. The point has plenty of both.

The point's first resident arrived in 1880. Jack Nibbe, Civil War veteran and recipient of the Congressional Medal of Honor, paid a $10 filing fee for a general homestead allotment of 160 acres, and $1.25 per acre for an additional 5.5 acres.

His property stretched from Point White northward along the shoreline for more than a mile. Nibbe took a Native American wife, had two children, and built a store just south of what later became the Point White community dock. Two of the large maple trees Nibbe planted were still standing at the site at the beginning of the twenty-first century.

According to early settlers, Jack Nibbe

Opposite: Ferries Come A-Calling
They called it the Point White dock, but it was up north about a quarter of a mile from the point. In fact, Crystal Springs had two docks. The dock in the lower photo was replaced by a fishing pier. The dock in the upper photo was farther north and called Gibson's Landing where Mosquito Fleet ferries provided connections to other parts of the sound.

Shirley and Gil Haight

Warren Lea Gazzam
Crystal Springs's best-known resident, Warren Gazzam was a speculator, ferry owner, and rake. His picture, taken by famous photographer Edward S. Curtis, is in Seattle's Rainier Club.

was a jovial, friendly man, and he became one of the island's first real estate salesmen. He divided his property and began to bring new settlers from Seattle in his little sloop to buy "west-side waterfront with plenty of sun to grow a garden."

He also carried the mail between Seattle and the point, helped supply fledgling farms, and was everybody's friend, said a descendant of one of the early settlers.

"When Janet Montgomery arrived from Scotland at the age of 19 to marry Alexander Munro, Nibbe ferried her across from Seattle," said Ralph Munro, grandson of Janet and Alexander Munro. "She was terribly frightened of the 'wild Indians' that she had read about in the European newspapers.

"As Nibbe put her ashore to settle in a new home, she said to him, 'What do I do now?' Nibbe laughed from the deck of his boat and shouted back, 'You better hide in the brush! The Indians will get you.'

"Of course she soon learned that the native peoples were very friendly, and she lived at that site for the rest of her life, raising ten children."

After a "colorful career at the point," Nibbe moved across the water to Sidney, which became Port Orchard, and later moved on to Bremerton, reports Elsie Frankland Marriott in *BAINBRIDGE through bifocals*.

The community was left without a post office until an ambitious promoter named Warren "Colonel" Gazzam moved there in 1904.

Charles Syversen bought out Nibbe in 1883, and Syversen and his

BIHS 3776

The Road to Crystal Springs

Crystal Springs has moved over the last hundred years. The dock, left, was Gibson's Landing on early plat maps, named for early resident James S. Gibson. Crystal Springs was farther north on property owned by Warren Gazzam, who had a dock of his own. Later, everything between Point White and Westwood was considered Crystal Springs.

wife began producing an astonishing crop of daughters. Charles Olaf Lindquist, who also moved to the island in 1883, paid $475 for thirty acres along the beach the following year. About the same time, a Captain Gibson settled north of the point and built a dock, which residents called Gibson's Landing.

A mile or so north of Gibson's Landing, the Ninninger family bought land that was blessed with several springs. They called the area Crystal Springs. Alas, history did not preserve their first names. In 1886, the area had only nine families.

"A one-room school was built in 1885," Katy Warner reports in *A History of Bainbridge Island.* "Only nine girls and five boys attended this little school." Directors were Lindquist, Syversen, and Ninninger.

In 1888, Alexander McKenzie Munro, a Scottish stone mason, arrived in Seattle just after the city went up in flames. Munro and his partner, Donald McRae, "built the Bailey Building . . . at Second and Cherry while Seattle was still smoking from the fire of 1889," his son James said.

In 1890, Alexander Munro asked Janet Montgomery, his school teacher sweetheart in Scotland, to come to Seattle, promising she could return home if she didn't like the Northwest. They were married October 2, 1890, and bought seven and a half acres half a mile north of Point White where they spent the rest of their lives, raising ten children and flocks of grandchildren. His work took him all over the Northwest.

"All of us children were born here with the exception of George who was born at Latona when Papa was cutting stone on the buildings of Denny Hall at the University of Washington," said James Munro.

Janet Munro accompanied her husband to Canada while her brother Lachlan Montgomery, a ship's carpenter at the Port Blakely mill, watched the kids.

"When Papa and Mama went to Victoria for the building of the Parliament Buildings and to New Westminster for the building of the government buildings there, Lachie (as we called him) came home to take care of the property," James Munro wrote.

The Munro kids got to witness the end of an era.

"My earliest memory is of being on the beach and watching the Indians from northern Puget Sound going by on their way to Puyallup to pick hops," James Munro said. "They put their mongrel dogs ashore at Agate Passage and the dogs ran on the beach until they picked them

The Stanleys of Point White

In 1901, William Stanley built a Victorian mansion on the point. It burned in 1918.

up at Point White and went on their way to the hop fields."

Duncan Munro, James's older brother, had similar memories.

"The Indians would paddle their canoes past and camp on the Point," he said. "We kids used to go down and visit them. We got along fine. Sometimes there'd be as many as twenty canoes camped there. They used to fill gunny sacks with clams and sell them for $2 or $2.50 each and ship them off to Seattle. They'd ship 20 or so sacks at a time. Later people would try to run them off, but they couldn't."

Lachie Montgomery helped the Munros with projects.

"When Duncan wanted to start a grocery store, Lachie and Papa built a store for him," James Munro said.

Just before the Great Depression, George Munro married Betty Troll, who was teaching at the Pleasant Beach School. When hard times came, they converted the store, which was across the road from Gibson's landing, into a house and raised three boys there. Their son Ralph went on to become Washington's secretary of state and one of the state's longest-serving officials.

"We had a great life in that little house," Ralph Munro said.

The last building that Alexander Munro cut stone for was the state Capitol in Olympia, says his obituary, published in November 1933.

In 1897, the Munros got new neighbors. Marie Hansen, widow of a ship captain, brought five of her six children from Norway to Bainbridge Island. Her son William and his wife Hilda purchased ten acres for $275 on the south side of the Munros and raised a family.

Marie Hansen's son Charles married Sadie Syversen, one of the seven Syversen girls. Captain Syversen gave each of his daughters a building site on the water, and Charles and his bride went to live there.

Toward the end of the nineteenth century, the job picture improved for South Bainbridge residents when the Bremerton shipyard got under way. Hardy Crystal Springers would row to and from work. In the summer, George Munro lived in a tent in the woods at Manette.

Point White residents multiplied rapidly. The souvenir booklet for Crystal Springs School's 1902 commencement lists twenty pupils. Included are four Cooks, three Hansens, three Munros, and two each of Johnsons, Prices, and Syversens, along with kids named Bates, Fuller, and Lindquist.

Near the end of the nineteenth century, Point White got one of its most affluent residents. On July 17, 1897, the steamer *Portland* arrived in Seattle carrying nearly $1 million in gold dust and nuggets along with the sixty-eight men who had wrested it from the gravel bars of the Yukon River. Only one was from Seattle.

"William Stanley had gone to the Yukon the year before and was coming home with $90,000 in gold; he had left two husky sons to guard a pair of claims in his absence," writes Nard Jones in his 1972 book, *Seattle.* "Obviously he intended to get richer."

He did. Stanley invested in land—on Capitol Hill in Seattle and in Pasadena, California. He also bought up all of Point White and built a huge three-story Victorian showplace overlooking Rich Passage, with a round turret that served as his daughter's playroom.

BIHS 563

The Syversens and Their Girls

Captain Charles J. Syversen homesteaded land on Crystal Springs Road in 1883. He gave each of his seven daughters adjoining lots, where they all returned with their families to live.

"The ranch had concrete root cellars, a three-story concrete barn, a rifle range, large orchards, and the usual assortment of [animals]," one of his descendants said.

The house burned down in 1918. Remnants of the barn remained on the hillside above the homesite at the end of the twentieth century.

In 1901, the area considered to be Crystal Springs was farther up the beach than it was a hundred years later. A plat map calls the half-mile-long stretch north of Point White "Gibson." Another mile north of that was Crystal Springs.

Warren Lea Gazzam, an Alabaman who assumed the honorary title of "Colonel," came to the island in 1904 after spending several years running an art gallery in Seattle and injecting himself into the social set there. He was a member of the prestigious Rainier Club, and an Edward Curtis photograph of him hangs on its paneled halls along with other early members.

The Colonel had a stern bearing and talked incessantly. He was also a go-for-broke real estate speculator, who was broke as often as he had money. He put together a transportation system, called the White Collar Line because of the distinctive white stripe around his steamers' smokestacks. The steamers connected the West Sound region to Seattle and other ports.

But the colonel was also a notorious ladies' man, who reputedly told his young bride on their wedding night that "as a Southern gentleman he could not be expected to be faithful," according to Andrew Ward, writer and radio commentator who in 1989 bought Gazzam's former house.

Reid Hansen

Crystal Springs Elementary School
Teacher Hanna Tvete's students in 1910 were dominated by Munros, Edenharters, and Hansens. Top row: Willie Price, Jeanne Hansen, George Munro, Marie Dickjose, and George Edenharter. Middle row: Unknown, Harry Hansen, Allen Oakes, Edgar Kronholm, Fred DeSoto, and Bill Garthley. Front row: Allen Greenough, Connie Edenharter, Rose Edenharter, Ernest Kronholm, Margaret Garthley, Euphemia Munro, Isabel Munro, and Willie Hansen.

Gazzam built the house in 1905, an impressive six-thousand-square-foot showplace "of niggardly construction" out of beach rocks and timbers, according to Ward. The living room and adjoining dining room stretched sixty feet from one end to the other and "became the island's premier ballroom," Ward writes in an *American Heritage* article.

Gazzam named the house after his native Alabama, but island residents have called it the Gazzam House, no matter who owned it.

After the Gazzams had moved in, he and his wife Lizzie, whose nickname was Lulu, set up a post office in the house.

"The post office was across the bay (at Illahee) from our house and my father managed to get it transferred over to our side so we had

mail," his daughter Ruth Gazzam Haight said. "My mother was the postmistress, and we had the post office in our hallway."

The Stanleys down on Point White "were quite angry when we built a bigger house (than theirs) because we then had the biggest house on the island," Haight said.

Gazzam was seldom home, and the postal duties fell entirely on

The Lindquists

BIHS 3384

The Lindquists were another pioneer mainstay of the Crystal Springs area. Their Victorian home still stands near the former ferry dock that later became a community fishing pier. One of Jack Nibbe's maple trees is still there.

Lulu's shoulders. She rowed across the Port Orchard Narrows to Illahee to pick up the mail. Lulu earned a place in island history in her own right. According to Ruth, Lulu went to Victoria, B.C., and brought back seeds of a tall yellow-flowered plant for her yard. They were scotch broom, colorful but smelly, that islanders have been fighting

ever since. Lulu may not have acted alone. Marriott says "some Catholic Sisters brought with them some roots of it at the time they founded their convent in Old Steilacoom" that may have spread.

The Colonel had big plans for Crystal Springs. He bought five hundred acres on credit and subdivided the beachfront north of his estate, calling it Westwood.

"His intention was to line the shore with summer cottages of his Rainier Club pals, and to that end he founded a mosquito fleet, called the White Collar Line, that zigzagged up and down Port Orchard Channel," Ward said.

Gazzam didn't exactly "found" a mosquito fleet. He bought into a one-boat operation started by Captain John Hansen and his sons in Poulsbo and, after the captain died, helped the family buy out a competitor, forming the Kitsap County Transportation Company, according to Carolyn Neal and and Thomas Kilday Janus in their book, *Puget Sound Ferries,* published in 2001.

Gazzam's move assured reliable transportation to Westwood, until his small fleet got bought up by a larger company and then went out of business. Residents of Westwood had to find another way to get to town.

"These Westwood people built their own road when the boat service was removed, because they did not want a public road cutting across or in front of their properties," Marriott writes. "It cost them *plenty,* both to build and to maintain."

Gazzam's company was first to introduce diesel-powered ships to Puget Sound. But he sold out in 1917 to the Puget Sound Navigation Company after a ruinous battle for cargo, landings, and passengers.

Gazzam was still vice president of the combined company when on October 5, 1917, its steamer *Tolo* was rammed and sunk by a tugboat named *Magic.* Gazzam was aboard. So were Jeanne and Harry Hansen of Crystal Springs, along with fifty other passengers and a crew of eight. Jeanne and her brother had to don life jackets and jump into the frigid water. Gazzam didn't get his feet wet. He threw a plank between the sinking ship and the tug and walked to safety.

"Take a last look at the old *Tolo,"* Harry shouted to his sister. Turning, she saw the smokestack sink below the surface.

"It was like watching the earth disappear," Jeanne Hansen Cook

First school bus

John Munro, in the driver's seat, operated the island's first school bus to transport Crystal Springs kids to Winslow High School for the princely sum of $7 per day. His contract required him to "furnish a suitable conveyance equipped with comfortable seats and . . . top and side curtains which shall be used during stormy and inclement weather."

Many Munros

Munros and neighbors gathered on the porch of the general store the Munros ran near Gibson's Landing about 1910, lower left. Top row: Ellen Helstrom, Duncan Munro, Harold Hansen, three Japanese visitors from a visiting boat, Lachlan Montgomery, and Alexander Munro. Bottom row: Mary and George Munro, Angus McLeod, William Munro, Harry Hansen, Joann Nelson, William Hansen Jr., Anjanet Munro, and Jenny Hansen. Attending a gathering forty years later, below, were George, Isabel, Duncan, Euphemia, D. Gordon, their mother Janet, William, Mary, Anjanet, James, and John.

BIHS 3423

BIHS 3387

BIHS 3415

Hansens Afloat

The Hansens were among the Scots and Norwegians who bought land at Crystal Springs. Here, the Hansen clan motors away from the Crystal Springs dock just across the road from their home, which was next door to the Munros. Left to right: William Jr., Hilda, William, Harry, Margaret Garthley, Jeanne, and Chris.

recalled when she was eighty-six.

The two, boarding students at Queen Anne High School, were returning to spend the weekend with their parents, William and Hilda Hansen.

The tug lowered a lifeboat and began tooting an SOS to a nearby steamer, named the *Kennedy,* whose crew fished out the Hansen kids.

"I didn't even lose my shoes," Jeanne Hansen Cook said. But three other passengers drowned, and one died of exposure.

Lulu, tired of Warren's absences and sexual escapades, divorced him in 1924. When the Depression hit, Lulu could no longer afford to live in the old house. Her daughter suggested making it a hotel.

"In 1932, Ruth's family moved to Bainbridge Island after foreclo-sure of their home in Seattle," said Ruth's son, Gil Haight. "In 1933, Lulu offered the Gazzam House as a domicile for Ruth's family. Ruth accepted on con-dition she could 'pay her own way,' and the 'summer hotel' was born, bred and managed by Ruth."

Ruth and her family lived in the barn

"Lulu became a house mother at either a sorority or fraternity at the U.W. in Seattle," Haight said.

The Colonel's creditors repossessed the house in 1939 while he was operating the Enetai Inn, a hotel in Bremerton. Ward says the Colonel had the dubious distinction of being named a co-respondent in a divorce case at age ninety-one. He died in 1967 at age ninety-seven.

94

BIHS 3774

Shirley and Gil Haight

BIHS 3773

The Gazzam House

One of Bainbridge Island's most imposing homes was built by real estate and transportation magnate Warren Lea Gazzam in 1905 at what was then called Crystal Springs, between Westwood and Gibson's Landing. The first floor was taken up with large living and dining rooms, which could be opened up to make an enormous ballroom. The house later served as a post office and, in the 1930s, a summer vacation inn. The outside walls are covered with beach stones that still show the marks of barnacles. Subsequent owners have had to spend great sums to upgrade the interior walls, wiring and plumbing

Gazzam Lake

Warren Gazzam's 500-acre estate included a lake over the hill east of the house that served as a kids' playground in both summer and winter, sometimes with tragic results. Several drowned. Two girls, upper left, try a make-shift raft. Reid Hansen, lower left, was a frequent skater in his teens.

Forest of Masts

*After the Hall Brothers Shipyard moved to Eagle Harbor in 1903, it became a magnet for tall ships from the entire
Pacific region that needed repairs and other work. A four-masted lumber schooner, far left, sits on the firm's cradle.
The Madison Avenue dock is in the left foreground. Note the clear-cut hill behind Eagledale in the right photo.*

Cramped Quarters

The steep north shore of Blakely Harbor left precious little space for the Hall brothers to build the large four- and five-masted schooners for which they had become famous. In 1902, the firm began building a new shipyard in Eagle Harbor that would allow it to handle larger ships.

Chapter Ten

The Hall Brothers

None of those who have written about Bainbridge Island has been able to decide exactly what to do with the Hall brothers. They carved a unique niche in island history.

During their long career, the Halls—Henry, Winslow, and Isaac—designed and built some of the most majestic lumber and freight carriers that ever sailed the oceans. Their efforts helped build the Northwest lumber business and placed Washington in the vanguard of states that developed trade with nations around the Pacific Rim. They started in Cohasset, Massachusetts, and ended up in Winslow on Bainbridge Island.

Because most island and Northwest histories—including this one—have listed their subject matter by community, the story of the Halls has made a clumsy fit in any spot, simply because they didn't stay in one place. But they made their mark wherever they landed.

Little survives of the Halls' activities in Port Ludlow at the northern neck of Hood Canal. Andrew Price Jr. covers the Halls' twenty-year stay in Port Blakely in his book, *Port Blakely: the Community Captain Renton built.* After their move to Winslow in 1903, the shipbuilding and repair institution the Halls built survived into the twenty-first century.

"Isaac and Winslow Hall were two of the fifteen children born to George and Cynthia Collier Hall of Cohasset, Massachusetts," Price writes. "Propelled, perhaps, by numbers, six boys in the family sought opportunity on the West Coast. James, the eldest, sailed to California in 1844. He was followed by brothers Isaac, Abraham, Samuel, Winslow G., and Henry Knox Hall."

Isaac and Winslow got jobs at the U.S. Navy shipyard at Mare Island in San Francisco Bay, established in 1854.

"It was from this employment that Isaac and Winslow left to start their own firm at Port Ludlow in 1873," Price says. "They called it 'Hall Bros. Shipbuilding Firm,' a title usually shortened to 'Hall Brothers.' Henry Knox Hall joined them there in 1875."

To be close to their lumber source, the Halls picked a spot near a small sawmill operated by a man named Arthur Phinney. They already had discovered that Douglas fir made ideal lumber for ships.

"The Halls were certainly attracted as well by the length of the timber to which they would have access, a single old-growth fir often providing the full keelson of a good-sized vessel," Price says. "The wood was easy to work and planks easy to shape to the designer's plan.

"During the seven years they operated the shipyard at Port Ludlow, the Halls built thirty-one vessels. The sugar plantations in the Kingdom of Hawaii were undergoing a period of very rapid expansion in the 1870s, and somehow the Halls were able to capitalize on this expansion."

Price says Winslow Hall was probably the firm's chief designer. He moved from Port Ludlow back to San Francisco to manage the firm's operations there.

Phinney, the mill owner, died in 1877, and when Pope and Talbot

BIHS 1042

Winslow G. Hall, 1833-1898

bought the mill and shipyard site, they wanted to expand the mill, forcing the Halls to look for a new location. One obvious possibility was in Port Blakely near Captain William Renton's big mill.

"To Captain Renton, it made sense to try to attract the firm to Port Blakely," Price writes. "So he set about trying to persuade Isaac and Henry to make the move. By way of incentive, Captain Renton offered to make land available for the shipyard east of the company houses reaching out toward Blakely Point.

"He also agreed to build a railroad track along the waterfront from the mill to the yard for the movement of timbers and planking. He even agreed to build five houses above the yard, on what became known as Halls' Hill. These were for the Halls and their senior people."

In 1879, the same year Isaac Hall died, the Halls took Renton up on the offer. The move brought boom times to Port Blakely.

"Naturally, there was great excitement in Port Blakely," Price writes. "The shipyard would become a major addition to the town's employment base, boosting it soon by seventy and later by as many as one hundred forty men. New homes, beside the five on Hall's Hill, and new dormitories had to be built."

Building a shipyard on the steeply banked north shore was a major engineering feat. Workmen began sinking pilings along the shore in 1879, and the yard was completed in 1880.

"The lines of piling reached from well above the high tide line down to below the low tide line," Price recounts. "Thus, the ways were over two hundred feet long. The ships were built entirely above the high tide line in 'stocks' over the upper end of the ways so there was no interruption of work at even the highest tide. To the uninitiated, the ships appeared gingerly balanced on the ways with a high probability that each one would tip over as it slid down the ways into the harbor; but that never happened."

Price includes in his book a description of the yard prepared for the U.S. Census Bureau in 1881. The Hall yard was one of eleven similar shipyards on Puget Sound, the bureau noted.

> The owners have fitted up the Port Blakely yard at considerable expense and have sent a delegate to Bath, Maine, to report on labor-saving appliances there employed and to purchase steam saws, planers and a full line of equipment for their yard. Their schooners are fast, handsome

BIHS 1217

James Hall and His Father, Henry Knox Hall, Circa 1903

Ribs to Spare
*A new sailing schooner takes shape on the Hall brothers' ways in Port Blakely as
workmen install bracing for the massive ship's ribs. The shipyard's smoke stack can be seen through the
open bow. Said to be the West Coast's best shipbuilder, Hall produced a four-master in six to nine months.*

and popular, and have long, sharp bows, with slightly hollow lines, the top sides having a faint curve home, and at the stern round in sharply over the arch-board in a strikingly graceful fashion.

There is not a straight line on the surface of the hulls anywhere. . . . The average length of stuff (the planking) is twenty feet longer than that of eastern yards . . .

In 1882, the Hall brothers launched the 700-ton *Makah.* It was the fourth ship built at the Port Blakely yard, and the largest by a wide margin of anything else the yard built during the first eight years in its new location, according to Michael Jay Mjelde, maritime historian.

Like other Puget Sound builders, the Halls stuck at first to traditional square-rigged ship designs. Square-riggers worked well for long voyages but were not well-suited for the lumber trade, Price reports. They required large crews for sail-handling and lots of ballast when they were empty. Winslow Hall had a better idea.

The Schooner *Bainbridge*
The Halls launched the 566-ton Bainbridge *in 1900, one of thirty-eight four- and five-masted schooners the firm produced.*

"Winslow Hall was largely responsible for the design of the lumber schooner that carried only fore-and-aft sails and sometimes was outfitted with topsails above them," Price reports. "Such a ship required a significantly smaller crew than the old square-riggers, barks and barkentines. The crews were reduced further still with the advent of the steam donkey engine in the early 1880s. It aided immensely in hoisting the sails, raising anchors, and in working the bilge pumps."

Price cites the praise of sailing ship authority John Lyman, who said, "The Hall-designed lumber schooner had the additional advantage of requiring little or no ballast. . . . Newcomers to the trade were amazed at the way a lofty barkentine (or schooner) could stand up

102

empty with only a few tons to put her in proper sailing trim."

The Halls launched their first three-masted schooner May 1, 1881, followed by fifteen more over the next seven years, in addition to a bark and five barentines, Price reports. One was named for William Renton and launched in 1882.

The ships the Halls were turning out were, of course, vital to the Port Blakely mill for hauling lumber to its customers along the West Coast and other ports.

The Halls also built several steamers at Port Blakely but there wasn't much of a market for them at the time. In 1888, they launched their first four-masted schooner, which became the firm's "stock in trade." They built fifteen more over the next five years and completed twenty-seven by the end of the century.

Last Three Hulls for Blakely   BIHS 1796
As the new shipyard was being built in Eagle Harbor in 1902, the Halls continued work on ships in Port Blakely. The ship at left is the H. K. Hall, *launched May 24, 1902. It was their hull number 104.*

As the company gained confidence, Winslow Hall's ship designs kept growing larger. But in 1898, Winslow Hall died at age 65.

The following year, the firm launched the *Winslow G. Hall* in his honor. In 1902, stretching the Port Blakely yard's capacity to its limit, the firm launched a five-masted schooner measuring 1,237 tons and named for Henry Hall.

The *H. K. Hall* and two other five-masters of similar size could carry 1.5 million board feet of lumber, "a full week's output of the mill there," Price reports.

It was time to move. Steel-hulled steam-powered ships were the future for the industry. The Hall dynasty itself was in disarray. Henry

Knox Hall, 77, and his son James were the only ones left. But they launched into the new yard with vigor, buying up half a mile of waterfront in Eagle Harbor.

"[The corporation's] purchase of 77 acres in the heart of the community created the general impression that this was the beginning of a new era," writes Elsie Frankland Marriott in *BAINBRIDGE through bifocals.* "Ground was broken on the new site on the 6th of July

[1902]. A large amount of money was expended in transferring and erecting the new plant, the total investment being about $300,000.

"The plant proper covered nearly fifteen acres, over which were spread a marine railway, machine shops, power house, sawmill and joiner loft for cutting ship timbers, a large gridiron, warehouse, and various other buildings and shipyard equipment. This plant was constructed on a much larger scale here at Winslow than at Port Blakely, in fact it was one of the largest institutions in the state.

"As a shipbuilding concern it was one of the largest on the Pacific Coast. The Hall Brothers Shipyards became world known. Mention has been made of it in several sea-faring novels."

Marriott's description is more enthusiastic than factual. Mjelde points out that, while the Hall shipyard was only doing repair work, the Moran brothers, who got their start building Yukon river boats on Rockaway Beach, had a larger yard in Seattle, which was building the battleship USS *Nebraska*.

The Halls' $300,000 investment would be roughly equivalent to $6 million in the year 2000.

They weren't alone in the venture.

Others involved in the new corporation included George Billings, San Francisco shipping magnate who managed several Hall-built ships; two principals in the Pope and Talbot Company, owners of the Port Gamble mill; and a man named John Hubbard, who got rich in the Alaska gold rush.

Together, they invested $140,000 in the new yard. Billings, the managing owner of the syndicate, helped finance the deal to assure access to good repair facilities for his shipping fleet.

Full Rigged Ship

Barkentine

Four Masted Schooner

Andrew Price, Jr.

The new firm was incorporated as Hall Brothers Marine Railway and Shipbuilding Co., reports James Warren, historian and columnist for the *Seattle Post-Intelligencer.*

But the new yard never lived up to the dream that the Halls had for it. Their first major construction project, overseen by James Hall as the yard's manager, was a financial disaster.

According to a paper by Michael Jay Mjelde and others, the first ship built at the new yard was the steam schooner *Norwood* in 1904.

"This was the undoing of James Hall and his father in the overall management of the shipyard because they had some unfortunate cost overruns," they say. "And apparently, Jimmy Hall was lacking in some management skills and, as a result, he was forced out in the actual management of the yard. They only got about $50,000 for building this specific vessel."

Henry Hall died in 1909.

The corporation sold the yard in 1916 to Captain James Griffiths and several associates, who renamed it the Winslow Marine Railway and Shipbuilding Company. World War I brought more activity, but it had very lean years afterwards.

Repair work was limited by the hauling capacity of its marine railway. The company boasted of being able to haul out a 4,000-ton ship but the firm suffered a couple of embarrassing breakdowns when it tried. While hauling out a steamer named *City of Puebla,* one of the hauling chain's 35-pound links broke as the lift cradle neared the top.

"The way that marine railway went backwards was like a roller-coaster!" Winslow resident Ray Parfitt told a friend years later.

Not only did the marine railway end up sunk in the water, but *The City of Puebla* ended up on the beach across the harbor at Eagledale after hitting two schooners along the way, Parfitt said.

"The yard was still essentially a wood-ship building yard, and as yet had not constructed one steel ship," writes Mjelde in a June 1983 article in the magazine *Sea Chest.* "Moreover, the repair facilities were limited in comparison to Todd's shipyard at Seattle, for example, which boasted two floating dry docks of 3,000 and 12,000 tons lifting capacity."

The Winslow yard finally got into the steel ship construction business in 1939, just in time to play an important part in World War II. The yard went from 100 workers in 1940 to 2,300 workers in 1943. Between 1941 and 1945, the yard built seventeen steel minesweepers,

2567
W&S

Harbor in Transition
The Halls shared Eagle Harbor with Native Americans and mill workers who lived in shacks along the shore that would later become a public park. A laundry also was reported to be among the waterfront dwellings.

twelve steel harbor tugs, and assorted other craft.

In July 1946, Winslow Marine ceased operations and leased part of the facility to another firm. The yard closed in 1959.

The state bought part of the property in 1962 to service and repair its fleet of ferries. The Halls' massive shipbuilding sheds were dismantled, and part of the land was sold off for a condominium project.

For a time, the property was also home to an office building known as the *Review* Building where the *Bainbridge Island Review* newspaper was published and the Winslow City Council met. It burned in the 1950s.

Review columnist Katy Warner praised the move by the state to continue the Hall heritage by using the shipbuilding facility.

"It is fitting that present-day ferries should seek this same haven," Warner writes. "It is well to remember that up until 1950, when the Agate Pass Bridge was built, Bainbridge depended on its water transportation and harbors for its survival."

In the Cradle

The Reuce *was the first ship to try out Hall's new marine cradle in 1903. The large gear-and-chain assembly, lower right, pulled the cradle ashore with power from an electric motor. The chain, which had links that weighed 35 pounds each, broke several times over the years. One cradle's occupant ended up aground in Eagledale.*

Seaplane Visits
In 1938, the shipyard's marine railway hosted a Boeing Clipper that had to be weighed after the firm had made modifications.

SS Roanoke
The passenger steamship SS Roanoke was one of the largest ships to use the Hall brothers' marine railway. This picture was used in a brochure advertising the cradle's 4,000-ton capacity when the firm was up for sale.

Here They Come

Above: *During World War II, it was the Seattle workers, above, who commuted to Bainbridge Island for jobs. Winslow Marine Railway and Shipbuilding Company employed 2,300 people during the war years, and the old Winslow ferry dock was hard-pressed to handle the flow.*

Right: *Shipyard managers hung a sign on the rigging of a new minesweeper to encourage faster production. They even posted patriotic signs about the shipyard on the fronts of Seattle stores.*

Bill Weld

Award Winners

Charles M. Sigle, right center, vice president and general manager of the Winslow Marine Railway and Shipbuilding Co., presents achievement awards to workers as a morale booster. The awards were frequent, and all recipients were photographed, with prints handed out to local newspapers. The yard built seventeen minesweepers, repaired damaged warships, and converted civilian ships for war duty during World War II.

The View from the Crane

The yard's huge overhead crane provided photographer Bill Weld with a commanding view of the bustling shipyard.
A minesweeper's stern can be seen in the lower left-hand corner and another ship's mast is on the right.

Bill Weld

Minesweeper Heads Out

Bill Weld

A Winslow-produced U.S. Navy minesweeper in camouflage steams out of Eagle Harbor for sea trials at the height of World War II. Lifelong island resident Bill Weld, upper left, was the shipyard's chief photographer, who photographed the ships as they were launched and later got his own picture taken at the helm of one of them.

Bill Weld

The Ferry Is In

Eagle Harbor and Winslow were about to undergo major changes when this was taken about 1950. Commercial Ship Repair, successor to Winslow Marine, was still repairing ships. The white building between the large shed and the ferry dock housed Winslow City Hall and the Bainbridge Island Review *newspaper. Land had been cleared, left center, for Highway 305 to connect the ferry dock, right, with the new bridge across Agate Passage.*

Opposite: Assembly Line

No sooner was one minesweeper out the door than workers began setting a new keel in place for the next one. The jagged stump, lower left, is the remnant of the steel plate that was cut to launch the new ship seen out in the harbor.

Stumps and Pumpkins

During the 1880s, the village on Eagle Harbor known as Madrone was dwarfed by Port Madison and Port Blakely. It did have Eagle Harbor Congregational Church and a school, left photo. Riley Hoskinson home-steaded much of the land in the photo above. The dirt track bisecting the photo became Winslow Way. In 1903, the town changed its name to Winslow and became the island's economic center.

The West's First Weather Station

Kansan Riley M. Hoskinson homesteaded 160 acres in Madrone in 1878. The dirt track in front of his home later became Winslow Way, and Vern's Winslow Drugs later was built where his house stood. Hoskinson built the first weather station west of the Mississippi River, the square tower in right center, and took meticulous readings until 1899. He was also one of the island's first photographers. He took this picture in 1885.

Chapter Eleven

Winslow

In its time, Port Madison became a regional economic center and died. Port Blakely became a bigger center and lasted longer, but it died, too. Winslow, however, became the business, cultural, and governmental center of the island without a dominant industry.

Its beginnings were unpromising. Port Madison dominated the north end of the island, and Port Blakely, the south. In the middle, there were farms and stump ranches.

"The town of Winslow, now the largest on the island, has grown slowly on a plan quite opposite of that of both Port Madison and Port Blakely," Elsie Frankland Marriott writes in *BAINBRIDGE through bifocals,* published in 1941. "In the early mill towns, the communities were supported almost entirely by the mill companies. When the mills were through, the towns were through. At Winslow was a community which supported its enterprises."

Marriott reports that in 1874, a logger discovered a six-foot-thick coal vein on the shore of Eagle Harbor. He

BIHS 110

The Hoskinsons in their Garden

and other speculators grabbed up the surrounding land, but the vein petered out. Eagle Harbor's first resident was a man named James Ryan, who settled in what was then called Hawley, between Madrone and Wing Point. In 1878, Riley M. Hoskinson homesteaded 160 acres right in the center of what is now downtown Winslow.

"Mr. Hoskinson was from Kansas, as was Ambrose Grow, who followed in 1881, and took the adjoining section to the westward," she

writes. "Almost before he had established himself and family, Mr. Hoskinson started a weather bureau. The Department in Washington, D.C., called him a 'voluntary observer.' From February 1878 until February 1899, he gathered weather observations from a platform on top of his house, and sent his reports regularly to Washington, D.C. His records for the first twelve of those years are the only ones in existence for that period, since the bureau in Seattle had not yet been established."

They called the town Madrone.

By 1881, they had a one-room schoolhouse on the east side of Madison Avenue just north of the new Eagle Harbor Congregational Church. In 1890, Marriott reports, the town got its own post office. Mrs. Cynthia C. Williams was the first postmistress.

"Up until that time, the settlers had obtained their mail from Port Blakely, by means of rowboat to the south side [of Eagle Harbor] and then through a crude trail slashed through the woods over the hill to the mill," she says.

Katy Warner, island historian and newspaper columnist, reports that the Rev. John Damon, first pastor of the Congregational church, had a major influence throughout the region.

"He was called the 'marrying parson' because he went from place to place all over the Puget Sound area and conducted weddings," Warner writes in *A History of Bainbridge Island.* "Couples wishing to marry had to wait for Rev. Damon to come to their community and perform the wedding. Sometimes he married two or three couples in one day. The couples never knew for sure when he would be back again so they made their plans to fit into his visits."

When the town outgrew the one-room school, residents built a larger one across the street on what would become Winslow Green. Marriott says both schools were the community's gathering place. Residents held Lyceum meetings and gatherings of the Sons of Temperance, Good Templars, and a Masonic Lodge.

On the waterfront, D. S. Harris built a pavilion, dining room, and picnic ground where Madrone residents celebrated Independence Day.

"People from around the sound brought their children, pitched a tent, and remained for a summer vacation," Marriott says. "This pavilion was later used as an oakum loft."

Madrone might have spent decades as a sleepy little farming community if it hadn't been for the problems the Hall brothers were having building ships down in Blakely Harbor. They were running out of room.

"Five-masted schooners like the *Inca* and the *George E. Billings*," Henry Knox Hall said, "were the largest that could be built at the Port Blakely yard."

"To remain in business," Andrew Price Jr. says in his book, *Port Blakely: The Community Captain Renton Built*, "the company had to be able to build larger ships, mostly steamships. Furthermore, a better ship-repair facility was needed, and a drydock could not be built in the already crowded Port Blakely site. Neither was a location beside a large sawmill any longer key to the success of a shipyard as it had been in 1880. More and more ships were being made of steel. Larger storage areas were needed, and steel could be shipped to Eagle Harbor as easily as to Port Blakely. Steel ships were heavier than wooden ones, and new ship ways needed to be built."

Hall was also losing its leadership. Henry Hall was 77 in 1903. Isaac and Winslow Hall had started the company at Port Ludlow in 1873. Isaac had died in 1879. Winslow Hall, the company's chief designer, died in 1898 before Henry Hall decided to move the yard.

Winslow's Population		
	1940	1947
Winslow	669	905
*Bainbridge Island (winter)	3,000	4,000
*Bainbridge Island (summer)	6,000	7,000

*Estimate
Source: *Washington, A Guide to the Evergreen State*

Out of gratitude for the coming boost to its economy, Madrone's residents agreed to change the community's name to Winslow to honor Winslow Hall. Henry Hall built a twenty-room home in town. Other executives built homes on Ericksen Avenue, Marriott reports.

Real estate prices soared overnight. But with the new dreams of a commercial supremacy, (we are informed by Mr. Harry Wallace, one of the pioneer grocers of Winslow), the old spirit of social good-fellowship was gone. Even though there was already a Good Templar's Hall across from the school, two new halls were constructed, one considerably north of the shipyard. The other was built just west of Captain Kunkler's home. This last mentioned, and the newest of the three halls, was a two-story structure with kitchen, dining-room seating 200, balcony, and stage with full set of scenery.

Like all community projects, this one was accomplished by means of subscriptions, and the furnishings were donated. This third hall would have been a credit to a community four times the size of Winslow; but—'pride goeth before a fall'—it burned to the ground before the cost of building had been liquidated. The second hall, being in financial straits, was turned over to stockholders, and finally razed.

Community gatherings then went back to the Good Templar's Hall. Even church bazaars and dinners were held there because of the general feeling that the church was not the proper place for 'clapping' and laughter. This building now [in 1940] belongs to, and houses, the Winslow Public Library, and is also used for the services of the Christian Science Society of Winslow.

Before the Halls moved to Eagle Harbor, town residents decided the only way to solve their transportation problems was to build their own steamer.

"They built their own 'ways' and constructed the steamer *Eagle*," Marriott writes. "Then the *Florence K* was built in Tacoma and the eventual outcome was the Eagle Harbor Transportation Company."

Bad luck, however, dogged the *Eagle*.

"Money was raised to build the *Eagle* by selling shares in it," Warner reports. "Miss Jessie Billings sold the most shares, and she had the honor of christening it. Instead of breaking a bottle of champagne

Winslow Wash

Sadie Woodman, Winslow's postmistress, takes a walk across what we call the Ravine. But in 1900, they called it the Wash, a creek bed east of Ericksen Avenue that separated Winslow from Hawley and Wing Point.

BIHS 397

Madrone Store
*Percy Henderson came from Britain to Bainbridge Island around 1900
and started a store on the Eagle Harbor dock at the foot of Madison
Avenue. He took orders in the morning and made deliveries in the afternoon as far north as New Brooklyn Road, way out in the farm belt.*

The early steamers docked at the foot of Madison Avenue at a landing on which Percy Henderson's store was built. Warner also reports that Captain B. F. Kunkler, skipper of the *Eagle* before its demise, built a newspaper plant near the dock and produced a paper called *The Beacon.* It lasted three years.

Winslow also got street lights and a volunteer fire department, but the street lights didn't last very long. They were discontinued after about five years "because of lack of interest, and the burden of expense on a few families."

"In 1929, a volunteer fire department was organized, but this venture, because of lack of interest, was also short-lived," Marriott wrote in 1940. "Fire-fighting equipment was purchased but was never used. It is still stored—probably without fire insurance; while the 'bucket brigade,' consisting of as many volunteers as live within a radius of the smell of smoke, aided by a 'draft list' called by 'Central,' [the local telephone operator] goes into lively action."

Winslow Wash, the ravine that ran north from the harbor through the heart of Winslow, created a major impediment to commerce until townspeople built a bridge across it.

"It was hard for the horses and buggies to go through this steep gulch," Warner writes. "It didn't make for easy walking either, so two separate little business places were built on each side of the gulch.

"On the west side of the gulch there was the church, the school, the grocery store, and the steamer dock. Across the gulch on the east side, Charlie Brehmer built a butcher shop. It was a little frame building. Next door to the butcher shop, the Nakatas built their home.

"Mrs. Nakata started a barbershop in her home. She cut most of the men's hair as well as the children's. Near these two places, Mr. Wyatt had a bakery. On a lot east of the butcher shop, the Winslow

over its bow, Miss Billings scattered a bouquet of flowers. Many old-timers did not like this idea and said that it would bring the *Eagle* bad luck. The *Eagle's* first trip was a free ride for all of the people to Port Madison. After the *Eagle* arrived in Port Madison it had engine trouble. The passengers waited aboard the steamer for four hours while its boiler was fixed."

Winslow residents got two years of service out of the *Eagle.*

"Then on an August night in 1902, she burned to the water's edge while tied to the dock," Warner says. "No one knew how the fire started. But the 'badluck' prediction seemed to come true."

120

Downtown Winslow, Looking West

BIHS 1017

After the Halls moved their shipyard to Eagle Harbor in 1903, Winslow's business picked up considerably. This picture was taken from atop a water tower across Winslow Way from the Winslow Hotel. The two-story building, foreground, later housed the Bainbridge Island Chamber of Commerce.

Hotel was built. The hotel was built by the Hemrich Brewery in Seattle. They felt it would have a large business because it was near the shipyard."

Warner reports that two sisters, Margaret Bradley and Katherine Clements, rented the hotel, remodeled it, and began serving lunch to the shipyard workers.

"A path led from the hotel to the shipyard," Warner says. "Some workers lived in the hotel, but at lunch time most of the men ate at the hotel whether they lived there or not. When there was a big job at the shipyard, the hotel was not large enough to take care of all the men. The men would have to rent rooms from the townspeople. But they would eat at the hotel. No one commuted in those days as the steamer service was too inconvenient."

The hotel burned in 1924.

After the Port Blakely mill closed, the shipyard in Winslow was the island's only major industry. Many former mill workers turned to agriculture instead. Several entrepreneurs on the south end of the island built elaborate glass hot houses to grow fresh produce that was shipped daily by ferry to Seattle's markets.

Winslow-area residents turned to strawberries.

"The bulk of the strawberries raised on Bainbridge Island is processed at a cannery at Winslow, about a mile west of the main town, called the Winslow Berry Growers Association," Marriott writes. "This enterprise was established in the early 1900s. At first, the fruit was canned in the home of S. Sumiyoshi. Then in 1923, the cannery

was built. By 1932, this cannery building was entirely outgrown, necessitating a new structure 110 feet by 225 feet, on the old location.

"The one popular method of preservation is the freezing of the berries in small containers. During the strawberry season, two hundred employees, among them many housewives and school girls, share in a $15,000 payroll. The entire output of the cannery, which in 1940 amounted to 1,981,035 pounds, is handled by R. D. Bodle Company of Seattle."

Winslow's first permanent brick building was put up by Walter Keys in 1929, Warner reports. It sat on the north side of Winslow Way just east of Madison Avenue and housed Puget Power and a drug store. There was no commercial development on the south side of the street.

"Up to this time, the land on the south side of Winslow Way was heavily wooded," Warner reports. "It was full of blackberry bushes and underbrush. Trails were made through this area by people going to and from the ferry dock.

"A neighborhood picnic grounds was on the site of the present Town and Country Supermarket. This property was not developed until 1946. Then Herbert Allen built a department

BIHS 138

Winslow's First Post Office
Madrone got its first post office August 11, 1890. When the town changed its name to Winslow in 1903, Sadie Woodman was postmistress. The post office building later was moved to the back of the lot west of the ravine on Winslow Way.

store and post office on the corner of Winslow Way and Madison Avenue."

Allen's development spurred other entrepreneurs, she says. Walter, Henry, and H. E. Anderson built a hardware store and grocery next to Allen's department store. The merchants formed a club known as the

Winslow Boosters, Warner writes, which promoted improvements.

Before World War II, Winslow's economy was fairly stable. The shipyard and creosote plant, which began operating in 1905 on the south shore of Eagle Harbor, provided jobs, and many families supported themselves by raising berries and garden produce for the Seattle markets. A small fishing fleet took up residence in the harbor, and the fishermen built houses in Eagledale.

The island's road system, however, remained primitive. Many residents used their own boats or depended on local steamers for transportation to other parts of the island. By 1940, several dirt or gravel roads made it possible for someone to drive a car around much of the perimeter of the island. According to a state guidebook published in 1941, the island had 24.7 miles of roads and "stage service to main points on the island, 10c[ents]. Numerous cabin camps and cottages. Graveled roads encircle the island."

The guidebook lists Winslow's population as 669 persons. The town of Creosote across the bay had a population of 250.

The *Bainbridge Island Review* and its editor, Walt Woodward, made international headlines when Woodward defied U.S. secrecy policy in August 1941, reporting the arrival of the British battleship *HMS Warspite* in Puget Sound waters. The crippled ship had been hit by a bomb during the defense of the island of Crete in the Mediterranean and was sent to Bremerton for repairs. The Roosevelt Administration was trying to keep secret the extent of U.S. support for the British in the months before the United States entered the war.

When the country did enter the war after the Japanese attack on Pearl Harbor, Bainbridge Island was thrust into a major role as gatekeeper for Bremerton's front door. The island also played a major role

BIHS 1018

Rooms to Let
When Margaret Bradley and Katherine Clements ran the Winslow Hotel east of the Wash, they fed lunch to most of the shipyard workers, whether they lived there or not. The hotel burned down in 1924.

as a communications and listening center for the entire Pacific.

World War II brought more people to Winslow as work increased at the shipyard in Eagle Harbor. The vacant, brush-covered land between Winslow Way and the harbor was cleared for housing.

"During the war years, there was virtually no unemployment," writes Reid Hansen, native islander and Crystal Springs resident in a Bainbridge Island Historical Society newsletter article. "The creosote plant was running at full steam. The Winslow shipyard was turning out minesweepers and repairing other ships. It was easy for a teenager to get a job at the shipyard after school and during the summer.

"People commuted to Seattle for their jobs and to Bremerton to work in the Bremerton Naval Shipyard. . . . Often, the huge ships were anchored between Illahee and Crystal Springs for degaussing.

Busy Dock
Madison Avenue's dock was a center for commercial activities, including gasoline storage and shopping.

City Council
Winslow's council after incorporation in 1947 included, from left: Harold Woodman and Dr. Frank Shepard, council members; William Roberts, treasurer; Herbert Allen, mayor; Ray Williamson, George Townsend and Edward Loverich, council members; and David Myers, clerk.

The Doctor Is In
Legend has it that Dr. Frank Shepard was the first islander to have a car, a Model T Ford, seen parked in the south portico of the magnificent home he built in 1922. It was on Madison Avenue about a block north of Winslow Way. The patient entrance was under the portico. The house was moved closer to the street and converted to offices in the 1990s.

BIHS 4263

First Drugstore
The Morrill Building at Ericksen Avenue and Winslow Way housed the island's first drug store and gift shop. It was built about the time that the Hall brothers moved their shipyard to Eagle Harbor in 1903.

BIHS 152

Celebrating the Fourth

Winslow has been celebrating Independence Day for more than a century. Stuart Hoskinson shot this in 1897.

"Beachcombing was very lucrative because of the many items that were thrown or lost overboard. This, along with barrage balloons and other naval activity, made life very interesting living along the shore."

The island's agricultural community was disrupted in March 1942 when the U.S. government suspended Constitutional rights for Americans of Japanese ancestry. The 275 Japanese American island residents were transported to "internment" camps.

After the war, many didn't return. The thousands of military personnel and defense workers were gone. Some Japanese American families who did return found their homes and businesses neglected or destroyed. Many had to start over. Winslow had many new problems.

In 1947, the Winslow Boosters asked residents to approve a plan to incorporate Winslow as a fourth-class city.

"The Winslow people had mixed feelings. . . . Some were for it.

Others were very much against it," Warner writes. "The election was held on Saturday, August 23, 1947. The move to become a town won by only twelve votes. One hundred nineteen people voted for it, and one hundred seven voted against it."

Herbert Allen became Winslow's new mayor. William Roberts was named treasurer, and David Meyers was elected clerk. Council members included Dr. Frank Shepard, Harold Woodman, Carl Pratt, Pern Clifton, and Ray Williamson. Four months later in another election. Pratt and Clifton were replaced by George Townsend and Ed Loverich.

Winslow's life changed again changed dramatically when, in 1950, the new Agate Pass Bridge connected the island with the Kitsap Peninsula, bringing more tourists and customers.

Winslow's strong commercial base had won it the stability that Port Madison and Port Blakely were never able to achieve.

BIHS 3148

Celebrating the Centennial

Above: *Bainbridge Island residents celebrate the Grand Old Fourth with one of the zaniest parades in America. Anyone can join in. In 1953, the annual trek down Winslow Way marked Washington Territory's 100th anniversary, and many participants dressed in pioneer themes.*

Right, *Ralph Munro, 10, and his dog Jip paid tribute to those who arrived by covered wagon. Fifty years later, a kilt-clad Munro still was participating in the parade, leading a Scottish pipe band. The parade, sponsored by the Bainbridge Island Chamber of Commerce, attracts tens of thousands of onlookers from throughout the region.*

BIHS 3151

Bring on the Traffic

BISD

The Madison Avenue-High School Road intersection had little difficulty handling traffic in 1949. The high school, upper left, is off by itself. Commodore School, center had room to grow. Ground had just been cleared for St. Cecilia Catholic Church, across the intersection from the Church of Christ Scientist. The rest is berry fields.

Three-Story High School

BISD

Bainbridge High School had three levels when it was built in 1927, but several students set fire to it May 26, 1976. It was rebuilt and expanded several times to serve more than 1,000 students, filling in the entire area between the site of the old building and the school next door.

Winslow High School Class of 1926

BIHS 1527

Located at Madison Avenue and Winslow Way, Lincoln School provided class-rooms for both high school and grade school students, with some high school classes held across the street, until a new high school was built in 1927.

Lincoln School's Class of 1926

BIHS 170

Same school, same year, but these are the fifth and sixth graders at Lincoln School, which sat at what later would become Winslow Green. Elementary grades took over the whole school when the big kids moved out in 1928.

STRAWBERRY FIELD AT WINSLOW WASH.
DELIVERY TO R. D. BODLE CO.

Delivering the Berries

Otohiko Koura prepares samples from his berry fields at Madison Avenue and High School Road for commercial buyer R. D. Bodle in the late 1920s. The men are standing in the middle of what would become the Bainbridge Public Library. High School Road is the dirt path running east along the upper left corner.

Wing Point Guards Eagle Harbor's Entrance

BIHS 407

*Nearly every community had its own dock at the turn of the century. In this early photo taken from the Ferncliff area looking east,
Wing Point's dock juts out in the distance, and Creosote's dock can be seen in the upper right corner. The dock in the foreground was
built by a man named Hawley, who died before he could develop land for a summer home tract between Winslow and Wing Point.*

Chapter Twelve

Wing Point/Yeomalt

Wing Point can call itself home to eagles, one of Washington's most powerful U.S. Senators, and a recreational institution. It takes its name from the birds that got there first.

Its neighbor, Yeomalt, became home to Eagle Scouts and their brothers, and to members of the Young Women's Christian Association.

Great numbers of "Bald-headed Eagles" used to nest on the north point of Eagle Harbor, Elsie Frankland Marriott says in her book, *BAINBRIDGE through bifocals*. She speculates that their presence probably inspired the men in Charles Wilkes's Exploration Expedition to give the bird's name to the harbor.

"'Wing' and 'Bill,' being parts of an eagle were given to the north and south points of the harbor," she says, but in a footnote, she admits there were other opinions on the subject.

"Historians have given various reasons for applying this name to the harbor—all of which are more or less far-fetched," she says. "The oldest pioneers have testified that the eagles were there—from Wing Point to Hawley—year after year."

The northern, or "wing" point of the harbor was home to a large Native American settlement when white settlers began inspecting the island for homesites. After George Meigs had gotten his lumber mill going at Port Madison, Asa Fowler, who bought tracts of timber in several places on the island, including Pleasant Beach, set up a logging camp on the point. The first actual settlers on Wing Point, however, were the James Ryan family who, with Ryan's nephew, Charles Williams, moved into the old logging camp April 6, 1877. Then it became the "Ryan place," Marriott says.

MOHAI Seattle Post-Intelligencer

Warren G. Magnuson

Williams married Mrs. Ryan's daughter, Cynthia, and they homesteaded 160 acres on the point. But the point's most creative early dweller apparently was a man named Ebersole who built an "odd rambling house."

"He was a great reader," Marriott reports, "and a man with an inventive turn of mind, which was expressed in the unusual design of his home. The front of his living room was circular and of colored glass. There was a spiral stairway ascending to the second story, and in the dining-room, 'a ceiling like an ocean wave.'

"On top was a small lookout room resembling the pilot house of a ship. Mr. Ebersole attempted to build a tide mill in the lagoon on the beach, but that was not successful."

His home was later bought by the Antoncich family, which remodeled the oddly shaped house but retained some of the colored glass.

Because there were no roads on the point in those days, people had to "walk the beach" to get to town or elsewhere, Marriott says. In 1905, Fred Fisher built a dock from the south end of the point out into the harbor.

Around the turn of the century, James Hall of the Hall Bros. Shipyard bought the Ryan homestead and resided there for a time. He sold it to a man name Hawley. About 1924, Hawley built a long dock into Eagle Harbor and planned to plat the property for a summer home development. But he died, and the project went nowhere.

"Although Mr. Hawley never lived on Bainbridge, this locality still bears his name," Marriott says.

The point attracted residents who enjoyed recreational activities.

Wing Point Circa 1900

Wing Point was a stark cliff in this photo, taken from a boat. The point was owned by Mr. and Mrs. Charles H. Black Jr.

Wade Garretson

Everything has a beginning . . . and you might say the beginning of Wing Point Golf was in 1902! Some may argue for 1903 and others for another year, but the Scott Fitzgerald types who summered on the Point around the turn of the century scooped a few holes in the apple orchard for their first "game" in the vicinity of our present 7th tee.

It was the summer of 1902, according to Mrs. Connie McMicken. . . . <u>She was here!</u> (Mr. and Mrs. Maurice McMicken, affectionately known as "Mickey and Connie," have the longest continuous membership in both the original Wing Point Golf & Country Club and its successor, the present Wing Point Golf & Country Club.)

By 1916, the Wing Pointers of the time became more serious about golf and developed more of the orchard and meadow property into a six-hole course, most of it skirting the lower portion of the present course, south of the county road (Wing Point Way). In 1920, they incorporated the original Wing Point Golf & Country Club with capital of $10,000, which a few years later was enlarged to $15,000. They were now able to enlarge the course to a 9-holer and to build a clubhouse in 1925 (which was situated just east of our present 7th tee).

The course had sand-greens which some of our old-timers still mumble about. Apparently it wasn't St. Andrews. But the clubhouse? It became headquarters for some of the most convivial merrymaking the next 37 years ever knew!

"In 1910, a group of individuals played golf between the fruit trees, and then there was born the idea of a golf club," Marriott writes. "In a couple of years, Mr. Henry Rudow, the father of the idea, sold property to this group for a six-hole course. In 1916, the Club House was built and the course enlarged to nine holes."

Wing Pointers dispute both of those dates.

A semi-official history of the Wing Point Golf and Country Club says it was formed nearly a decade earlier. Here's an excerpt from a club publication called "Golf Among the Apple Trees."

The club later installed grass greens and built a modern clubhouse that included an outdoor swimming pool, locker and shower room, and a restaurant-meeting room that would become a center for island-wide gatherings.

Wing Point's best-known resident was seldom there. U.S. Senator Warren G. Magnuson owned a comfortable home at the tip of the point with a sweeping view of Puget Sound from Mount Baker to Mount Rainier.

Magnuson, born in 1905 in Minnesota, earned a bachelors degree from the University of Washington in 1926 and graduated from the

Joan Wilt

Playing Through the Trees at Wing Point Golf Club

Members included, from left, Richard Hayter, Jim "Fritz" MacDonald, Harry Woods, Eugene Rudow, Carl King, Mrs. Henry Rudow, Steve Antoncich, Henry Rudow, Dorothy MacDonald, Frank Machlein, Margaret Machlein, and Anabel Hayter.

UW School of Law in 1929.

Two years later, after serving as a special King County prosecutor, he was elected to Washington's House of Representatives. He was 28. Magnuson, a Democrat, went on to the U.S. House of Representatives in 1937, and in 1944, he resigned to accept an appointment to the U.S. Senate after the resignation of Homer T. Bone. He stayed in the Senate until 1980 when, old and feeble, he was defeated by a Republican former attorney general, Slade Gorton.

During his forty-five-year career in Congress, Magnuson sponsored legislation to build Grand Coulee Dam and establish the federal power system on the Columbia and Snake Rivers. Other legislation he pushed funded the National Institutes of Health. Magnuson wielded some of his greatest influence during whiskey-and-poker sessions with Presidents Franklin Roosevelt, Harry Truman, John Kennedy, and Lyndon Johnson, according to Shelby Scates, former *Seattle Post-Intelligencer* reporter

Fore!

Wing Point Golf Club's first six-hole course had sand "greens," and most of it was south of the County Road, which later was named Wing Point Way. Hazards included trees, ditches, and fences.

who wrote a biography of Magnuson.

During a Seattle stopover around 1961, President John F. Kennedy paid tribute to Magnuson's quiet influence. "Maggie," Kennedy said, would shuffle into the Senate chambers, mumble a few words, and "the next thing you knew, Grand Coulee Dam was built."

After Magnuson lost his Senate seat, he lived out his final days in a suite at Seattle's Olympic Hotel, too infirm to visit his home on Wing Point. One of his most-quoted sayings was that "If I had known I was going to live this long, I would have taken better care of

myself."

He died in 1989 at age 84.

Another early resident on the point was Andrew Denny, great-grandson of "the father of Seattle," Arthur Denny, who led a wagon train of the city's founders to the Oregon Territory in 1851. The Denny party's presence helped justify the separation of Washington Territory from the land below the Columbia River several years later.

Just north of Wing Point was another point that became a haven for recreating Seattle residents. Yeomalt, known as "The Point is Wearing Down" by the island's first residents, was a popular beach

that Native Americans used for camping and fishing. Early white settlers, however, called it "Dead Man's Bar" because "the sea had cast ashore the remains of one of its unknown victims," according to Marriott.

"Mr. Finch homesteaded 160 acres near Dead Man's Bar, and early settlers from other parts of the island found Finche's[sic] Sand Spit, in the [1890]s, an attractive place to picnic," she writes. "About 1910, a number of young men from Seattle organized a club, purchased property, and built a club house."

They called their hideaway "The Yeomalt Club." Where they got the name has been lost. Being young men of some leisure and good education, they probably borrowed it from the Middle English term "yeoman," referring to "lesser freeholders ranking below the gentry."

Thomas D. Kelley, longtime Yeomalt resident, said he believes the name may have been derived from a Native American word meaning "dead man."

Shortly after the Yeomalt Club had been established, a man named Pettit began selling lots in a 180-acre subdivision west of the point that he called Rolling Bay City. Men from the club bought land from Pettit, and the area later became known as Ferncliff, Marriott reports.

As the club members established permanent homes, their interest in the club waned, and the property was sold in 1916. The new owners called it Yeomalt Lodge.

"At the present time [1940] it is operated by Mr. and Mrs. B. H. Pepys as a roller skating rink," Marriott says.

In 1912, the Young Womens Christian Association of Seattle bought eighteen acres north of Yeomalt Point. It ran a summer camp for girls and their families for several years, then abandoned it, Marriott says. The buildings deteriorated from lack of use.

"When I first saw the beach in 1952, the camp's large dining hall had collapsed and was a pile of lumber," Kelley writes. "There did remain a very nice counselor's complex above the beach. It was apparently built by a carpenter who knew his business, as everything, includ-

BIHS 738

Taking the Waters

Hardy bathers brave the chilly sound off Yeomalt Point's YWCA camp in the early days, protected by the heavy swimming garments of the time.

Family Outing
The Yeomalt YWCA camp's tent cabins could accommodate entire families. This photo was taken in about 1910.

BIHS 744

Chow Time
Diners had a choice of tables and chairs or stumps and logs in this gathering about 1915. Many of those who summered at the YWCA camp were from Seattle.

BIHS 745

ing the joints and logs, were perfectly arranged."

Kelley bought the property. He and his wife, Helen, made the cabins their summer home, and it became a gathering place for the Kelley clan for many years.

One of those was Kitty Kelley, author of a book on the British royal family called *The Royals* and other books. The Kelleys built a new home for their retirement years on the spot where the cabins had been but saved the original fireplace with the inscription, "YWCA."

Just west of Yeomalt, the Boy Scouts of America built a camp of their own, naming it Camp Hopkins for M. J. Hopkins, former British officer who organized Troop 1 in Rolling Bay, the island's first Scout troop. Scouts built a log cabin where troops could hold award ceremonies. An outdoor fireplace provided a place for campfires.

True to the Scouting tradition, troops were open to all island boys regardless of national origin. In 1942, when Japanese American families were forcibly removed from the island by Army soldiers, the troop pictured above lost one-third of its membership.

Hopkins came under criticism at the end of World War II because he backed a movement to block the return of Japanese families to their island homes. But they did return with the strong support of most of the community and the *Bainbridge Review*. The park was later renamed Camp Yeomalt.

During the 1950s, Camp Hopkins served as headquarters for a two-hundred-member U.S. Army unit that manned a Nike missile installation at Strawberry Park and another site in Eagledale with radar antenna and search lights.

The unit was part of the Cold War defenses for the Bremerton shipyard. Island resident Eddie Rollins served in the twenty-four man unit that operated the radar site.

"We went to Camp Hopkins once a week to shower," he said.

Boy Scouts Assemble

BIHS 827

Just up the hill from the YWCA camp was the Boy Scouts' Camp Hopkins, which featured a log clubhouse for troop gatherings. This photo, taken in 1941, shows a proud troop with an award. About one-third of this group's membership was of Asian ancestry.

M. J. Hopkins

The Log Lodge

BIHS

Camp Hopkins played a small role in the Cold War when the Army used it for troops manning Nike units.

The View from Manitou Beach

Murden Cove, Manitou Beach, Rolling Bay. Call it what you will, the bay north of Yeomalt Point has gone by many names, but it has one of the island's best vistas of Seattle, the Cascades, and Puget Sound. This view, taken by W. Jonnes in 1915, shows the Manitou dock and general store with the remnants of what must have been thick forest to the water's edge before it was logged.

Chapter Thirteen

Rolling Bay

Some of these first settlers sought other fields of endeavor, some we have as our neighbors and friends today, others have been gathered to their final rest. Now, after a period of twenty years, we later arrivals look across the Sound and see a city of a quarter of a million on the site of the town of thirty thousand. . . .

Our population has not increased as it should. We know there are many there who would welcome an opportunity of living in the country. Let us therefore work in harmony for their good and ours. They need to know of the advantages offered here, and we need their assistance in our civic and transportation problems.

—Fred Falconer Weld, 1911

Rolling Bay. That has to be one of the most picturesque community names in the Pacific Northwest. But that's not the name it began with. As in several other communities on the island, it took a while for residents to agree on a name, and names moved around.

Everyone knows where Skiff Point is. It's the first big bump you come to when traveling down the east side of Bainbridge Island. But where is Rolling Bay? One hundred years ago, the name referred to a different area than it does today. In a monograph written in 1910, Rolling Bay pioneer Fred Weld traced the community's beginnings back to 1876 when another pioneer, Dona Falk, homesteaded land near Skiff Point between Point Monroe and Wing Point.

He evidently saw the potential value of the shore lands lying around the harbor, as his claim included the fractional lots from what is now the west line of the (Skiff) Point property, west and south to the south line of section 14, or the north side of Rolling Bay City.

At this time logging operations had been carried on through the timber most easily accessible, the loggers taking only the finest of the trees. The timber that was left was later logged by others, who on account of the better demand

for lumber made more from their operations than did those who cut but the best.

The entire tract about the bay had been heavily wooded with fir, cedar, and hemlock. As may be imagined, it was a difficult matter to get through the woods except by the logging roads. The supply of timber seemed inexhaustible, and the land, after its removal, but of little value. Even as late as 1886, the timber on the Point property was sold to the Port Blakely mill at the rate of 1/2 [cent] per foot. In another generation these great impressive monarchs of the forests, with which the early struggled, will have become curiosities to be preserved and cared for.

Despite Weld's precise description, Rolling Bay City's location is difficult to pinpoint. But Falk got there first. According to Elsie Frankland Marriott in her book, *BAINBRIDGE through bifocals,* Falk supported his family by raising vegetables and berries, "which he carried by means of a neckyoke, and walked all the way to Port Madison to peddle his produce."

In 1891, not long after Skiff Point residents got homes built and fences up, they organized a Baptist church "with an original membership of 13," Weld says.

"The church was organized by one Cornelius Berg," Weld says. "Services were held at the homes of the members, chairs being carried from adjoining houses to furnish enough seats."

Descendants of Lium, Sorenson, Berg, Jacobsen, Johnson, Thompson, and Rodal clans still resided on the island a century later. Residents also organized a Ladies Sewing Society. Members realized quickly that the growing community needed a public hall and talked Ed Rodal into donating a piece of property, "and in 1909, by sales and subscriptions, built the hall that became the Rolling Bay Presbyterian Church," Weld says.

Weld describes how the community was named.

Bill Weld

Fred Falconer Weld

Rolling Bay Post Office
The first post office was built in 1892. At the end of the twentieth century, it was still in use.

BIHS 301

tolerated. So Rolling Bay was finally adopted because it began with an "R" and was <u>not</u> Rowles!

Transportation was a major problem for the little community. In order to provide a landing spot for local ferries, residents built a float out in the bay beyond the low-water mark just south of Skiff Point.

The community's first merchant, Weld says, was Frank L. Grow, "who in 1890 placed a small stock in a building on the waterfront owned by Mr. Soonis. The . . . venture was not a success and the store was closed three months later."

The community's economy was tied closely to that of Port Madison. Many men who had settled in Rolling Bay walked or rode to work on horseback. When the mill closed in 1892, families had to rely on what they could grow. Port Madison became a ghost town within a year. Some workers began commuting to Port Blakely.

According to Weld, Rolling Bay's first successful merchant was Charles Carlston, who built a store in 1901 at the end of the steamer dock, which he later sold

The post office was established in 1892. Up to this time the settlement had been known as Murden's Cove, or as Falk's Bay, or as Rowles Bay, the latter from the fact that a more or less undesirable squaw man of that name had camped on the now site of Mr. Falk's garden.

When it became necessary to choose a name for the post office, these names were all considered at a public meeting. Mr. Lium advocated the Norse name of San Weck, meaning a Sandy Cove—a very appropriate name.

The majority, however, wanted an "American" name, Captain Dickson fearing that any other might retard the application. The old name Rowles Bay was discussed, but the old fellow's reputation was such that that could not be

Free Delivery
Fresh out of high school, Luke Halvorsen delivered groceries on the east side of the island for Lucas Rodal in Rodal's shiny new truck. The store, located at the corner of Valley Road and Sunrise Drive, later became Bay Hay and Feed. Rolling Bay Post Office is next door.

Photo courtesty of Howard Block

One of the Best Views in the Territory
*The Manitou Beach General Store stood at the head of the steamer landing, which had been
financed by surrounding property owners to connect themselves with the rest of the world.
The store burned down and was replaced with a building that was converted later into a residence.*

to J. J. Arnot. Then in 1912, Lucas Rodal, opened a store up the hill at what would become Valley Road and Sunrise Drive. Rodal and Weld teamed up to develop an underground water delivery system in the community to replace the wells that frequently ran out of water during the summer months.

Obtaining a reliable source of good potable water was a problem in several areas of the island. Weld and his partner Jack Dovey, both civil engineers, surveyed the entire island and made a contour map of it in 1915. They didn't develop water systems in other areas, however.

They determined that the island's soil was all glacial till, ground down and deposited by the ice fields more than ten thousand years ago. Some areas had deep sand and gravel beds. Others had only shallow surface soil atop impermeable clay.

"Wells are hard to get in the Rolling Bay region because of the underlying soil conditions," Marriott writes. "Many early settlers constructed cisterns in which rain water was stored for use during the summer months. In dry seasons this supply was apt to become exhausted and water had to be hauled from the Grisdale creek until the fall rains came."

Rolling Bay's highest point, Marriott reports, was 380 feet above sea level on a hill "north of the old Rolling Bay Schoolhouse." Storage tanks, built on that hill just south of Wilkes Elementary School, fed water through pipelines to much of the island's north end for more than a century. Weld, who built his home on the bluff overlooking the sound, found a spring near the beach that could supply his home.

Then the community underwent another name change.

"In the years which followed, the area which was originally named 'Rolling Bay' became known as 'Manitou Beach,' and the name 'Rolling Bay' applied to all the district to the northward half way to Port Madison," Marriott writes. "By 1921, it surely seemed that Manitou Beach had a future. The dock was overhauled—new piles, new planking, a new waiting room, and new railing.

"A neat grocery was operating at the head of the dock, and across the road a butcher shop. Then, in 1937, after a futile effort to obtain a ferry service to Manitou Beach, all Bainbridge Island transportation service was centralized at Eagle Harbor. The Manitou dock was removed to Winslow. In 1939, Rodal Motors, across from the Rodal store (Central Store), gave this corner the appearance of a possible future civic center."

The name Manitou stemmed from a subdivision two real estate agents set up in 1907 on the old fifty-acre Jacobsen homestead at Skiff Point that had been platted by W. E. Parker, calling it Manitou Park.

"The name was chosen because of an ideal health resort in Colorado which bears the same name," Marriott said, "and because of the Indian meaning of the name in that locality, which is 'Great Spirit,' it seemed to Mr. Parker very fitting that this point which looks out constantly to Mount Rainier, the 'mountain that was God,' should also be called 'Manitou Park.'"

Manitou Beach
Early businesses gathered at the head of the Manitou Beach dock, one of the best and busiest on the island's east side. H. B. Adams, developer of Manitou Park, advertised it as "the front door of Seattle. The business man's home."

Parker also helped create one of Rolling Bay's major institutions. Marriott, borrowing from Weld, writes:

> About 1909, Mr. Parker built a summer hotel together with four cottages where the old Jacobsen home had stood. Then the hotel not proving a success, the grounds were leased for a couple of years to a NWW Chautauqua group. Those were gala days in the social life of the community while it lasted, but that venture also failed to provide sufficient income to meet expenses.
>
> Then in 1914, forty acres on the point were taken over for the founding of Moran Junior College. No more desirable location could be found for a boys' school than this wooded projection before which passes the traffic of the Seven Seas. The school at first occupied the hotel building. Later three large stucco buildings, with extensive grounds and an ampitheater, [sic] were constructed. In 1926, a postoffice was established at the school. One of the buildings, called "Wilson Hall," was destroyed by an explosion on November 9th, 1932.

According to another source, Wilson Hall housed a chemistry laboratory where someone left a Bunsen burner on while workmen were repairing a gas line. A fitting leaked, and gas filled air spaces inside the walls. When the gas spread to the chemistry lab, it exploded, blowing out the walls of the building.

The school was founded by Frank Moran, son of Robert Moran, shipbuilding pioneer and one-time mayor of Seattle. The Great

Depression reduced private school enrollments, and the Moran School closed in 1933.

Joe Hill, owner of an eponymous military academy in Portland, Oregon, bought the defunct school, and on September 15, 1938, reopened it as the Puget Sound Naval Academy. It was a school for boys between 12 and 18, designed to prepare them for entry into the U.S. Naval Academy or the U.S. Coast Guard Academy. N. N. Gates, retired Navy lieutenant commander and former Annapolis instructor, was its first headmaster.

The school operated during the war, and many of its graduates joined the Navy and Coast Guard.

Schooling became more exciting after the war. The Navy, with a surplus of used ships on its hands, gave several to the academy, including two "Ducks"—DUKH amphibious trucks—and a three-year-old, 136-foot-long minesweeper, designated the PCS-1400.

The vessel had been built in Newport Beach, California, and launched May 20, 1944, serving as a sonar training vessel until it was decommissioned August 19, 1947, and given to the academy, according to government records obtained by Charles W. Lindenberg, 1950 graduate of the academy. Bainbridge Island had its own navy.

When it arrived at Rolling Bay, no one at the school knew how to operate it. After dropping anchor, the Navy crew that delivered it shut down the ship's machinery and disembarked for shore.

According to Bill Weld, Rolling Bay resident who was working at the school at the time, one of the school's staff persuaded the chief machinist's mate in charge to show him how to start the engines and generate electricity for the other systems.

As a student, Lindenberg served as electrician's mate aboard the ship and wrote a fictionalized account of his days at the school, entitled *The Academy,* published in 1998. Lindenberg said he changed the names of his teachers and fellow students, but "98 percent of the story is true."

One of the academy's most memorable events occurred in June 1950 when the school's headmaster decided to let the students sail the ship to the Portland,

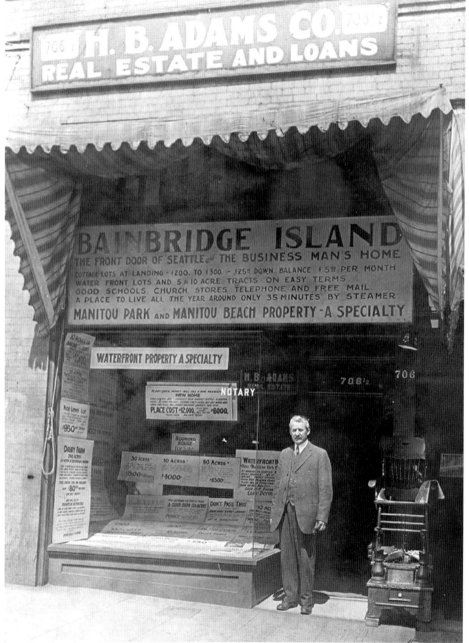

For Sale: Manitou Beach   John Adams estate
It was only thirty-five minutes to Seattle by steamer, according to H. B. Adams. He sold everything from lots to 80-acre tracts. "Cottage lots at landing, $200 to $300. $25 down, balance $5 per month. A place to live all the year around."

Oregon, Rose Festival.

A six-day roundtrip to Portland in a vessel that size was more daunting than it sounds. The ship apparently had no ship-to-shore radio, no radar, no sonar. The students weren't even proficient in Morse code.

As the ship was steaming up Puget Sound toward the Strait of Juan de Fuca, a U.S. Navy destroyer passed in the opposite direction. A signalman aboard the Navy ship sent the cadets a message with the ship's blinker, but no one aboard the minesweeper could understand Morse code.

The crew made it down the coast without incident, however, successfully crossing the Columbia River's treacherous sandbar.

As the students motored back up the coast after their visit, they were forced to shut down one of the ship's two engines because of a broken oil seal. Then, in the middle of the night, the crew missed the passage into the Strait of Juan de Fuca.

According to Lindenberg, a keyring on a crewman's belt caused the ship's compass to give a false heading, and the helmsman believed

The Moran School and Puget Sound Naval Academy
In 1914, the Moran Junior College took over forty acres at Skiff Point, the site of a former hotel and Chautauqua gathering place. The boys' boarding school had its own ferry landing. Another dock served Rolling Bay residents, who came down Gertie Johnson Road, upper right. The school became a maritime academy for boys in 1938, and it continued operations through and after World War II. In the 1950s, the facility was turned into a retirement center.

Popular with Swimmers

The Moran School's dock was busy in good weather. The large building, upper right, housed the school's chemistry laboratory.
Gas leaked into the walls of the building, and a Bunsen burner left on in the lab set it off, destroying the building.

they had rounded Cape Flattery and were heading for Port Angeles.

Seeing lights, they anchored for the night near the shore.

The next morning, they hailed a fishing boat and learned they had anchored off the west coast of Vancouver Island. The young sailors headed the ship back to American waters and returned home safely.

Students painted their ship white and took good care of it, Lindenberg said. The ship's only minor mishap occurred one windy fall when high winds caused the ship to drag its anchor, and it ended up aground on Skiff Point.

Academy staff members tried to slow the drifting vessel by dropping a second anchor, but its chain became entangled with the other anchor's chain. The Navy sent a crew out to cut one of the chains and haul the vessel into Eagle Harbor.

According to documents Lindenberg received from the Naval Historical Center, the ship was returned to the Navy on April 14, 1952, shortly after the academy ceased operations.

Thus ended the only documented period when Bainbridge Island was homeport to a warship.

On July 25, 1956, the PCS-1400 was "certified not essential to the defense of the U.S." and was sold March 14, 1957, to O. H. "Doc" Freeman, operator of a marine supply store on Seattle's Lake Union. He paid the government $18,776.76 for the ship and renamed it *Coquille.*

Its academic life over, the school became a nursing home.

Atten-SHUN!

*Their PCS-1400 shipshape, Puget Sound Naval Academy cadets muster in dress blues. The vessel
at the stern is a Higgins boat built to haul officers around. Photographer Bill Weld took the picture
from a DUKH, or Duck, one of two war surplus amphibious craft the U.S. Navy also provided.*

Point Monroe

Tom Thatcher

Lieutenant Charles Wilkes named the spit that forms the southern boundary of Port Madison after our fifth president, James Monroe, and the port's northern peninsula for our third president, Thomas Jefferson. Long a haven for beach dwellers and itinerant fishermen, the sandspit and the lagoon it shelters became a year-round residence for an increasing number of islanders.

Chapter Fourteen

Point Monroe

When we first came to the sandspit, it was just a long narrow piece of land with a few logs that had at sometime been washed up by the tide. There was a narrow road that zigzagged along the spit.

—Ida Thatcher

Charles Wilkes called it Point Monroe, the southeastern-most piece of land that defined the boundaries of Port Madison. Ask some where Point Monroe is, and you'll get a slack jaw.

To island residents, it has always been just the Sand Spit. Or Sandspit. Or just plain sandspit. Nobody but mapmakers calls it Point Monroe, the name Wilkes hung on it in 1841.

The sickle-shaped sandbar that sticks up like a wayward curl atop a moppet's head has a lively past as a summer playground and seasonal camp. Later, its closeness to the sea and spectacular unobstructed views looking toward the Cascade Mountains and Mount Baker collected hardy year-round dwellers who didn't mind the occasional storms and high tides that flooded their floors.

Before white men arrived, the sandy promontory teemed with shellfish. The warm waters of its shallow lagoon were ideal for swimming.

"The north (or Madison) sandspit was a camping place for the Coast Salish Suquamish tribe, and although it was used year-round, it was not a permanent village," wrote Gerald Elfendahl in *Times, Tides and Traditions,* a pamphlet published in 1990 by Point Monroe residents. "Because of the exposed nature of the spit, most of its use was probably during the spring and summer."

The Suquamish called it "Tce wi'tc (pronounced 'cawec') and it translates as outside or lying off-shore place," Elfendahl says. "The lagoon was called 'Tq ta'bats' or inside place. The head of the lagoon was referred to as 'Sal a'gwep' which means the place w[h]ere the butt ends of the trees are lying."

Wood for early habitations on the spit came from logs and lumber that washed up on the beach. One of Wilkes's surveying crews spent a night there in May 1842.

"The land in the vicinity of our camp was much lower than usual and thickly covered with pines a mile away. . . . We found the lodges of the Suquamish Indians, engaged in preparing their winter stores," wrote Lieutenant A. L. Case, skipper of the surveying ship *Vincennes.* "They told me this was a favorite resort of the Tribe, who were at times here in great numbers."

Case and crew "feasted that night on salmon brought by the men and boys they had visited."

After George Meigs started his sawmill in 1853, his lumberjacks cut the timber on the bluff "and a community of Chinese," who were employed at the mill as cooks, "resided on the point for a while."

"The lagoon was a favorite swimming spot for native and settler children, a trail connected the sandspit with Port Madison," Elfendahl says.

During the early years of the twentieth century, the sheltered lagoon attracted fishermen, who spent the winter months living on their boats or in shacks built from driftwood. Retired seamen and others camped year-round because fishing was good, and it was rent-free.

Then the spit's owners, M. R. and Georgie Wood, decided to make a subdivision out of it. Ida and Ken Thatcher had a better idea.

Ida Thatcher, former teacher at Pleasant Beach School who married Ken in 1935, had bought land in Port Madison in 1940.

"One day when we came to the Sand Spit beach, we saw the spit had been surveyed and staked out in fifty foot lots," Ida Thatcher said. "Ken . . . found that the Sand Spit was for sale. After much deliberation, we decide[d] to sell our Port Madison property and buy the Sand Spit, that is, the main part of it. . . .

"Ken remembered, as a young boy, hiking with his friends from Port Madison to swim in the warm water of the Sand Spit lagoon. It was like a private swimming pool for them as there were no people around, and the nearest house was the Fay's."

John Fay, a Seattle lawyer, and his family lived in a big two-story

149

FAY BAINBRIDGE STAT
MT. RAINIER - PUGET SO
#17916 - LIM

Tom Thatcher

Sun's Out

The Fay family's former beach drew big crowds after the state bought it for $5,000 and turned it into Fay Bainbridge State Park.

"Ken then offered Hank Larson the chance to join us," Ida Thatcher says. "Ken and Hank were friends and often fished together. Hank was working for his father, who owned Larson Lumber Yard at Pleasant Beach.

"Hank decided to join us as a partner, but most of our other friends thought we were simply crazy!"

Their only neighbors were a light and bell tower halfway down the spit, and "halfway from there to the tip of the spit was a white house" built by a man named Jack McDonald.

"There were no other buildings on the spit, except for quite a few squatter's shacks," she writes. "Many nationalities were represented by the fellows living here. One of the most colorful was a German, called Happy. His shanty, just around the bend of the spit, was built from logs and boards he found on the beach."

Fred Fontaine lived next to the bell tower "and it was his job to turn on the bell when the fog came in," Ida says.

The shack dwellers weren't the spit's only colorful things.

"When we first came, I remember the whole Sand Spit was covered with little lavender flowers, each with a little round lavender blossom at the top of a straight stem," she says. "I learned that they were wild onions. With all the fill dirt that has been brought in, they have all disappeared."

house on the bluff above the south end of the spit. His son later sold the property to the state for a park, with the stipulation that its name bear that of the Fays. In 1944, the state paid him $5,000 and named it Fay Bainbridge State Park.

To complete their sandspit purchase, the Thatchers needed a partner. Ken sold his brother Tom one lot.

-MONROE POINT-
-(THE SANDSPIT)-

Tom Thatcher

Safe Haven

The Sandspit protects boats in foul weather, but its residents must endure occasional storms and flooding from high tides.

In 1941, the Thatchers and Larson built summer cabins near the middle of the spit. It was Ken's "first attempt at carpentry."

"We had no water," Ida Thatcher said. "When we came we had to bring all our water with us. We had no electricity. When the cabin was complete enough for us to stay in it overnight, our gas lamp was our light. We cooked on a big woodstove like you see in antique shops."

The Thatcher and Larson cabins, much remodeled, were still occupied at the end of the twentieth century. In 1951, as more families moved to the point, the Thatchers built a year-round home down the beach, complete with utilities.

By then, however, much of the peninsula looked like a moonscape.

"There were large holes dug by people who had taken loads of gravel to build their basements, bulkheads, and swimming pools," Ida Thatcher said.

"I think people moving here today have the feeling that the Sand Spit was always like this. Not so!" she said. "It took lots and lots of pioneering."

151

Fletcher's Landing

BIHS 1092

The steamer Norwood *drops passengers from Brownsville across Port Orchard Bay on July 10, 1922, in this photo donated by Ruth and John Nelson. The pier was Bainbridge Island's main connection to the Kitsap Peninsula and later became the primary westward connection for car traffic. During the summer, Fletcher's Landing brought thousands of mainlanders to camp at Fletcher Bay and dance at Foster's Resort.*

Chapter Fifteen

Island Center

Greek George's? Thankfully, the name didn't survive, but the community endured. It became Island Center.

We in the twenty-first century think nothing of driving over the steep hills and valleys from Bainbridge Island's west coast to its eastern side. But bicyclists can attest to how steep those ridges are.

Because of our glacier-carved topography, the island's center was one of its remotest spots until economic demands were sufficient to justify the cost of cross-island roads. Like other neighborhoods, Island Center residents turned to the water.

Fletcher's Bay and Island Center developed as an alternative to spending half a day walking or going by horseback to Winslow to shop.

Fletcher's Bay, which attracted one of the island's earliest residents, proved to be an ideal location for a steamer dock, and it became the island's primary connection to the Olympic Peninsula. Here's how Elsie Frankland Marriott tells the story:

Fletcher's Bay was named for William C. Fletcher who entered a land

BIHS 107

Living Beauty

The Bainbridge Gardens float won first place in the second annual Bainbridge Island Fair, held in 1923 at the Island Center Community Hall. The driver is Zenmatsu Seko, who with his brother Zenhichi Harui established the gardens.

claim thereon July 17, 1869. Fletcher did contract logging for the mills. Later, Fletcher with his Indian wife and their children, settled at the north extremity of Pleasant Beach, where Andreason's Garage stands.

George Alap, a Greek squaw-man who also settled on the bay at a very early date, remained there until his death in 1892. For this man the bay was at first called "Greek George's." Alap was buried in front of his house on the shore of the bay, and years later when Mr. and Mrs. Cox purchased this property the body was exhumed.

Another early resident was Edward "Logger" Olson, Marriott reports. He homesteaded 160 acres in 1871 "farther north," probably up near the Tolo area.

"Logger Olson was from the rough and tough old school, but he was a good citizen and a good father, and together with his wife, reared three children, Daisy, William, and Emil, on this homestead," Marriott says.

But it was the Fosters, Erlandsens, Hamiltons, Sekos, and Haruis who put Fletcher's Bay and Island Center on the map permanently. Warner Foster and his wife set up a resort that drew people from

The Center of Island Center

BIHS 1255

Island Center Hall was and still is a center for island activities. Here, islanders attend a community fair in the 1920s.

throughout the sound. In *BAINBRIDGE through Bifocals,* published in 1941, Marriott writes:

> In 1911, Mr. and Mrs. Foster came to Fletcher's Bay and established a pavilion, picnic grounds, store, and camps—adjacent to the beach. The camps accommodating one hundred persons were filled each summer with people who made an exodus from the city to this cooling spot.
>
> Large organization picnics came by excursion steamers and the place became quite famous in its way. A post office was secured in 1915, and was operated until 1936. The ferry *Hiyu* began to ply between Fletcher's Bay and Brownsville on the mainland in 1924.
>
> In 1927, the Fosters moved back from the waterfront, and the Hamiltons occupied the waterfront location. The Fosters then built a large dance pavilion and landscaped the grounds. This place became noted— and still is—for the Schottische, the Svenska Polka, the Rhinelander, and the Hambone.
>
> They also established a small store on the road just opposite the pavilion. The Hamiltons also built a pavilion on the old Foster location, and there attempted to carry out the night-club form of entertainment. They also built cottages, and on the opposite side of the road, a gas station. Mr. Peter Erlandsen established a store near the approach to the ferry landing.
>
> On July 18, 1932, about three o'clock in the morning, the Hamilton Pavilion, three cottages, and Mr. Erlandsen's store were all completely destroyed by fire. The Ray Hamiltons barely escaped with their lives. The total loss was about $30,000. About a month later all was rebuilt with the addition at Hamiltons, of a bowling alley.

As development grew on Fletcher's Bay, another community was growing about a half a mile to the south and east. In 1878, Ida Anderson, daughter of the Hoskinsons of Winslow, and her husband had homesteaded in what would become Island Center.

"There was no highway then, only trails through the woods, over which lumber, chicken feed, and supplies were carried on the back,"

BIHS 478

Island Center School

Students engage in a rock-throwing contest in front of the Island Center School, built in 1882. When the island's ten school districts were consolidated in 1928, students rode buses to Winslow. The school building was moved in the 1960s and became the Bainbridge Island Historical Museum.

Marriott writes. "A year later, Samuel Sutter, the lath-mill foreman in Meigs's [Port Madison] mill, took a quarter section and settled a quarter of a mile to the north of the Andersons."

The early families grew rapidly, and their kids soon needed a school. And that's how the area got its name, Marriott says.

The school, which still stands and is used as a Community Hall, was built in 1882, on an acre of land donated by Samuel Sutter. This was School District No. 15. Later, Miss Annie Bucklin, a teacher, feeling the need of a Sunday school in the community, sent for Rev. Green, the

Sunday School Superintendent for the Territory, to organize one. It was at this time that Island Center received its name.

Finding themselves in need of an address to which Sunday School supplies could be sent, Mrs. Anderson said, "We're about in the center here, let's call it 'Island Center.'"

The Olson family also donated land for a cemetery in the area. Residents later built a larger community hall, and the old school was used for other purposes until it was moved to Strawberry Hill Park.

Marriott also recorded another addition to Island Center area.

155

Hanging Out at Erlandsen's

These bathing beauties enjoy the sun on the beach in front of Erlandsen's Store, a popular hangout in the 1920s. The well-to-do flocked to Pleasant Beach in the summer, and the working class used the campground on Fletcher's Bay.

BIHS 1024

Olson's family to trade food for land near Fletcher's Bay on which they built their gardens, store, and gas station.

With the impending internment in 1942, Seko and Harui were faced with the loss of everything they had built.

"But the wonderful thing that happened was that the grocery store was leased by some very wonderful people, and they paid rent, which paid the taxes," said Junkoh Harui sixty years later, "so it has been in our family name for ninety-seven years."

It was the Anderson family, probably descended from the Hoskinsons' daughter, Ida, who kept the store in business.

After the war, the brothers returned to the island to find their beloved greenhouses collapsed and the nursery destroyed. In 1989, Junkoh Harui was able to begin restoring the property to what his father and uncle had dreamed of developing.

A decade later, Bainbridge Gardens was a regional resource for those who love flowers, plants, and beautiful gardens.

This is what she has to say:

And, now, a lapse of time! About three-quarters of a mile to the north, at the head of Fletcher's Bay and not far from the old homestead site of the "Logger Olson" family, is situated the twenty-acre nursery, greenhouses, grocery store, and gasoline station of Mr. Seko, which is called "Bainbridge Gardens."

Pools and rockeries with Japanese landscaping make this place one of the island's Beauty Spots. Mr. Seko at first located on the New Brooklyn road and sold vegetables raised in a truck garden at his home.

When she wrote her book, Marriott had no way of knowing that the beautiful Bainbridge Gardens she describes would almost die after the U.S. government ordered the island's Japanese-American residents out of their homes and sent them to camps for most of the war.

Zenmatsu Seko and his brother Zenhichi Harui had lived on the island since the turn of the century, working first at the Port Blakely mill, then establishing a farm on New Brooklyn Road. According to Harui's son Junkoh, the brothers apparently struck a deal with Logger

Stores Galore

BIHS 1953

Foster's store and dance pavilion were popular gathering spots for visitors from Seattle and Bremerton during the summer.

Welcome to Bainbridge Gardens

Around 1910, brothers Zenhichi Harui and Zenmatsu Seko acquired land near Fletcher Bay and established Bainbridge Gardens. They started with a produce stand, expanded to a grocery and nursery, then added greenhouses and a sunken garden. This picture probably was taken in the early 1920s. The gardens went to ruin during World War II, but Harui's son, Junkoh, started a nursery in Winslow in 1958 and moved operations back to the original site of Bainbridge Gardens in 1989.

Downtown Eagledale

The Southside Grocery on Ward Avenue became the community's gathering place after Wiktar Lundgren established it about 1910. A telephone line can be seen running from the top of the building across to the other side of Eagle Harbor.

Chapter Sixteen

Eagledale

In the beginning, everyone just called it Southside, simply because it was on the south side of Eagle Harbor. According to Elsie Frankland Marriott, the harbor's first settler wasn't Riley Hoskinson, who filed a homestead on the north shore of Eagle Harbor in 1878.

"Around on the south side of the harbor, Taylor's logging camp was located in 1875," she writes in *BAINBRIDGE through bifocals*. "Mike Taylor, whose real name was 'Teelan,' was the first on Eagle Harbor to make legal claim to a homestead. Taylor Avenue is named for him.

"He located in the east part of what was, until recent years, called 'Southside.' The name was changed to 'Eagledale' by means of a contest, which was won by Ed Severson, who still wears $2.50 gold cuff links (Eagles), the prize for his selection of this name."

In those days, $2.50 was big dough. Pictures taken of Eagle Harbor in the 1880s show that Taylor and his associates were good at their trade. Hardly a tree stands on the south side of the harbor. The land was considered worthless without timber.

BIHS 558

One of the First

The Alanson N. Reeve house was one of Eagledale's first homes, but it burned. It was replaced by one still occupied at the end of the twentieth century.

On the heels of the loggers came the farmers and fishermen. "In 1881, Captain Saddler, a famous ox-yoke maker, bought land near where the creosote plant now stands," Marriott writes. "Previously this point had been planted into potatoes by a man whom the first settlers called 'Old Gus.' Mr. Glen Reeve came to Southside and settled in 1884, having first lived at Port Madison for six or seven years."

The Ryans, Hoskinsons, and Grows had farms on the north shore.

"In 1887, Captain Saddler started a brick-yard which operated for about five years, and this enterprise brought other settlers," Marriott says. "At first the children on the south side went by rowboat to Madrone to school, then Mr. Reeve opened his doors, and classes were held in his home.

"Later, Mr. Reeve's son, W. A. Reeve, built the little school back on the hill, which is now known as the 'Chapel.'"

Many of Eagledale's settlers worked at Port Blakely. One of the most successful was Malcolm McDonald, who operated the

McDonald School

This imposing structure was the center of Eagledale between 1905 and the 1960s. It was named for Malcolm McDonald, who donated the land on which it is built. The Port Blakely mill donated the lumber.

BIHS 559

yard, and, after 1905, the creosote plant on Bill Point.

Eagledale became a melting pot of nationalities. Many Swedish farmers occupied the higher elevations in what was called New Sweden.

Around the end of the nineteenth century, a fisherman named Carr came to Eagledale from a Whidbey-sized island in the Adriatic Sea off the coast of Croatia. He was joined in 1903 by Tom Loverich, who was from Losinj in the same area.

"A lot of Slavs who jumped ship were skilled at building boats and fishing," said Tom Loverich's grandson, Gary. "My grandfather owned two fishing boats."

Carr and other Croatians came from Dugi Otok, according to Sam Mirkovich Jr. Sam's grandfather Nick left Dugi Otok about 1907 and fished in Corpus Christi, Texas, before heading west, landing on Bainbridge Island about 1909.

Word spread to their relatives back home and to other Croatian fisherman, many of whom were distant relatives and from the same village of Veli Rat.

"It was a lot like back home for them," said Sam Mirkovich Jr. "Dugi Otok was larger but still very similar to Bainbridge Island. Villages were far apart, and people had to take a ferry boat to the city of Zadar on the mainland to do major shopping."

Eagledale also became home for other Croatian families, the Svornichs, Rerecichs, Ugleses, Uglesichs and others whose families have remained on the island into the twenty-first century. The fishermen among them used Eagledale as their home base, anchoring their boats in Eagle Harbor during the off-season. Soon there were so many Croats whose names ended in "ich" that neighbors across the water took to calling Eagledale "Ichville."

Men in Eagledale took jobs at the shipyard on the north shore and rowed to work. Eagledale fishermen would often bring their catches back home and sell them on the docks in Eagle Harbor. During the off-

Bainbridge Hotel at Port Blakely and owned the Pleasant Beach Hotel and Pavilion. McDonald was Eagledale's sugar daddy.

"The McDonald ranch, up on the hill, with a large house and extensive barns, had many acres under cultivation," Marriott says. "Mr. McDonald was known as one of the largest land owners in Kitsap County. He donated the land for the school house, built in 1905, which bears his name."

The school operated until the 1960s. After that, children were taken by bus to schools in Winslow.

Eagledale provided good farmland within close proximity to several sources of income. There was Port Blakely, the Hall brothers ship-

Classes of '36

The entire student body of McDonald School turned out for a photo shoot at the end of the 1936 school year. After the school closed, the students were bused to Winslow. Many of the children in this photo still are island residents.

season, the fishermen found other jobs.

"Granddad fished for salmon and herring in Alaska and Puget Sound," said Sam Mirkovich Jr. "In the wintertime when he wasn't fishing, he worked at the creosote plant."

Nick Mirkovich bought a house on Ward Avenue in 1911 and paid it off in a couple of years, his grandson said. The house was later remodeled with the efforts of the entire family. It remained in the family into the twenty-first century.

Sardines offered more financial return than salmon and herring. So the Mirkovichs turned their efforts that way in the 1930s. But they needed a larger boat, and they bought one called *Sonny Boy,* Sam

Mirkovich Jr. said. By 1937, with the encouragement of Nick's oldest son, Sam, the family had a new boat built in San Pedro, California. They named it the *Bainbridge.*

"The original plan was supposed to have been [an] 80-foot [boat] with a tophouse," Sam Mirkovich Jr. said. "But when it was being built, dad said 'Ah, it ought to be longer.' So he negotiated six feet in and the tophouse out, and the price was the same.

"He convinced the builder, 'Well, at least you can put a two-by-twelve plank up on the top for me to sit on.' And I think it was that way until just before the war, and then they put a tophouse on it."

161

Ichville?

In the early 1900s, Eagledale attracted Croatian fishermen with names like Svornich, Mirkovich, and Sarunich, prompting some residents to nickname Eagledale "Ichville." More than a dozen fishing boats homeported in Eagle Harbor.

BIHS 4044

Warner reports, a steamer almost destroyed the dock.

"The sternwheeler *Tourist* had been bringing people to the resort at Eagledale," she writes. "As she left the picnic grounds on her last trip back to Seattle, she missed her course. The *Tourist* was loaded with passengers, and she plowed through the center of the long dock.

"The steamer cut the end of the dock off from the main part of it. The dock was split in two. But no one was hurt and neither was the *Tourist*. She continued on her way but much work had to be done to rebuild the dock."

When Port Blakely's ferry service ended in 1937, "a new ferry dock was built near the old resort land [in Eagledale]," Warner says. "The Seattle-Winslow ferry made regular stops at this dock. Then it went across the bay to the Winslow terminal.

"A few years later the stop at Eagledale was discontinued and the ferries went only to Winslow."

Eagledale's dock played an important role in the island's economy. After the demise of the Port Blakely mill, several island entrepreneurs built massive greenhouses on the island's south end. Flowers and produce raised in the greenhouses were delivered to Seattle aboard steamers and ferries that landed at Eagledale and Port Blakely.

The Eagledale dock received international attention when, shortly after the beginning of World War II, the U.S. government ordered Japanese residents and their American-born children to move inland or be sent to "internment" camps. Bainbridge residents were first to go.

A *Seattle Post-Intelligencer* photographer shot a picture of the Japanese families and their friends walking down the long dock between a phalanx of soldiers carrying bayoneted rifles. Many of their Bainbridge Island friends walked with them. The photo ran in newspapers around the world. (See page 193.)

More than sixty years later, the boat was still in use. Sam's brother Richard was using it for fishing from Alaska to California, and the boat was still as sound as when it was built, Sam Mirkovich Jr. said.

Eagledale also had a resort.

"As more people moved to Eagledale and Creosote, Mr. Ed Seedin and Mr. Dunlap built a resort there," Katy Warner writes in *A History of Bainbridge Island*. "They built a dance hall, bathhouse, and picnic grounds at Eagledale Beach. Passenger steamers brought people to the resort in the summer time. But the resort was closed after a few years because it lost money."

The resort attracted people from all over the island and around the sound. To accommodate steamers, the resort developers built a long dock out into Eagle Harbor at Taylor Avenue. In the early 1920s,

Sam Mirkovich Jr.

Our Flagship

Nick and Kate Mirkovich, their three sons, and two sons-in-law formed a partnership in 1937 to have an 87-foot fishing boat built in San Pedro, California. Named the Bainbridge, *it has been in the family ever since. This photo, taken in the 1940s, shows a U.S. Navy aircraft carrier tied up at the Winslow shipyard. Croatian fishing families anchored more than a dozen boats in Eagle Harbor.*

163

Chapter Seventeen

Creosote/Rockaway Beach

At the end of the nineteenth century, the United States found it very much in its strategic interest to build a waterway between the Atlantic and Pacific Oceans.

But the job would require thousands of pilings and timbers for locks, docks, and piers. Where did the builders look for them?

Bainbridge Island.

And a few other places, too, of course. But they wanted the best. And the best were the Douglas fir logs and timbers that came from the Puget Sound region, treated with creosote and other chemicals to protect them from water and predators. Two Northwest businessmen saw a great opportunity.

"Piers and docks in the Northwest's warm marine waters have always been plagued by a whole host of enemies of wood: marine borers, fungi, and insects," says a history of the companies that the two men founded. "In the early days, green pilings were wrapped with burlap soaked in hot tar, but with only moderate success. A really effective means of protecting wood didn't become widely available until the late nineteenth century, when wood was pressure- and vacuum-treated with creosote, a coal tar product derived from making steel.

"At that time, two pioneers invested the capital and obtained the know-how to commercially treat piling, timbers, and railroad ties, and thus virtually put an end to the problem. These companies were the forerunners of the Wyckoff Company."

In 1884, J. M. Colman built a plant at the foot of a cliff along Seattle's waterfront that would later be called the Denny Regrade.

"Colman, a real estate developer and businessman, set up a vacuum- and pressure-treating facility and began selling treated pilings throughout the Seattle area," the Wyckoff history says. "He moved his plant to West Seattle in 1907."

It continued to operate there until it was forced to close eighty

Opposite: The Grandeur That Was Creosote

The community known as Creosote was a major development during the first half of the twentieth century. It provided treated pilings for major projects from the Panama Canal to the wharfs of Hong Kong.

years later by the U.S. Environmental Protection Agency.

One of Elliott Bay's largest piers was named in honor of Colman, and it became the main terminus for a ferry system that served communities throughout the Puget Sound region.

The other pioneer was Horace Henry, who in 1906 became manager of the Pacific Creosoting Company after his boss went down with the steamer *Titanic*.

"In 1905, the creosote plant, called the '[Perfection] Piling Preserving Company,' located on Bill Point," Elsie Frankland Marriott writes in *BAINBRIDGE through bifocals*. "This company had been established just one year at Port Madison and was moved to Eagle Harbor on a scow. . . . Soon after the plant was moved, the name was changed to 'Pacific Creosoting Company,' and the method of preserving was also changed."

At the time the plant was moved, Bill Point "was occupied by three or four fishermen's shacks and covered with blackberries," according to Edith Lundgren and Grace Haynes, settlers in the area. Henry turned the point into a major industrial operation and company town. He called it Creosote.

Commercial activity was not new on the point, however. The Moran brothers got their start building small boats just around the corner on Rockaway Beach in the 1880s. After the Alaska Gold Rush in 1889, the small yard, built above the high tide line, turned out a dozen river boats for use on the Yukon River.

The Morans moved to larger quarters in Seattle, and the beach was left to squatters. Locals felt it was too exposed to winds and too dark because the sun went behind the hill to the west shortly after noon. Many years later, it became prime real estate because of its panoramic view of Seattle and the Cascade Mountains.

Creosote employed about one hundred workers who lived either in a bunkhouse above the post office or, if they had a family, in row houses on the hill above the plant, Marriott says. One of its first contracts was to supply lumber and pilings to the American company that

Creosote, Wash.
These men aren't waiting for their mail. They live there. The combination post office and store included a bunkhouse and cookhouse for single men.

was building the Panama Canal, a job that lasted more than a decade.

"Many large consignments have been handled, among them the preparation of the timber used in the Panama Canal," Marriott writes. "Another was for 350,000 treated piles for the Milwaukee Railroad; still another was for 17,000 feet of green piling for use in flood control in Topolobampo [Mexico]."

"Henry's plant produced the timbers used by the Los Angeles flood control in the [19]20s and '30s. Both companies shipped treated materials to build wharves on San Francisco Bay, particularly after the great Earthquake and fire of 1906," according to the company history.

"As railroads expanded and moved west, they provided treated railroad ties for James J. Hill's *Great Northern* and *Northern Pacific* railroads and Seattle's first railroad, the *Seattle-Walla Walla*, a narrow-gauge line that ran eastward to the coalfields of Renton and Newcastle."

The town of Renton was named for William Renton of Port Blakely, who provided financing for the rail line that never reached its destination, Walla Walla.

Another early history describes the plant and town Henry built.

The steamer dock at Creosote extended out to the group of pilings on which the flashing beacon now stands. At the end there was a waiting room, painted red, as were all of the company buildings. The outstanding feature, however, was the railroad track and the little push cart which went with it. Its purpose was for transporting sacks of mail and boxes of groceries to the store on the land end. Every young boy was envious of the one who got to push the cart along the track, and of course the girls liked to ride.

Island residents in the late twentieth century tended to think of Eagledale and Creosote as one community. But in the early 1900s, they were separated by the deep ravine created by Taylor Creek, which runs into Eagle Harbor near the steamer and ferry dock near Creosote. Each had its own store.

In a memoir published by the Kitsap County Historical Society, Lundgren and Haynes describe the area.

The roads were of gravel for wagon wheels, but they were mostly mud puddles and wagon wheel ruts, plus dusty roads in the summertime. The South Side Dock was made of one big float, surrounded by piling to hold it in position and it was connected to the shore by a long float made of logs.

Part of the time it was under water and you had to jump from one piece of float to another to either get out to the big float or get to shore. Many passengers walked off the float and into the water on dark nights when they walked off the plank from the steamers.

In order to get to Creosote before the bridge was built you had to go down one side of the gully and across the creek and up to the other side by a trail. On long dry summers, due to lack of well water, this creek was a famous watering place for cows and horses.

According to a report prepared for the EPA on the plant's history, Creosote was believed to be one of the largest plants of its kind.

Vessels loading at plant of The Pacific Creosoting Co., Eagle Harbor, Puget Sound Creosote Wk. P.O.

Big Haul

The Pacific Creosoting Company was one of the world's largest suppliers of treated wood in the early 1900s, with customers around the world. The four-masted bark on the left was the Invincible, *taking on a load of creosoted pilings in 1910. Note the early steam freighter, upper center.*

A 1919 advertisement in a wood preservation industry document characterizes the company as "the Largest Creosoting Plant in the West," and announces "Piling, Mine Timbers, Cross-arms, Bridge Timbers, Paving Blocks, Railroad Ties, Conduit, and Stave Pipe" among the wood items treated at the plant.

Treated Douglas fir blocks, used for street paving and for the floors of some industrial machine shops, were manufactured in the paving block saw mill on the north side of the West Dock. Although the demand for wood paving blocks diminished with the advent of asphalt and concrete paving technologies, the saw mill remained in its original location until it was torn down in the mid-1970s.

Creosote's company store carried basic supplies for workers and families. Residents of the company town described living conditions in the nineteen four-room houses as "very comfortable," according to the EPA report, and said rent was "reasonable" at around $10 per month.

"Located west of the plant site on the other side of a large ravine

Company Houses

BIHS 4125

Company Houses

A side benefit for Creosote workers was one of the best water views in the Pacific Northwest, small compensation for the toxic fumes and noise.

was a public dancehall, frequented by married couples and single men," the report says.

"A bridge across the ravine provided access to the dancehall, which served the Creosote community as a roller rink until sometime in the early 1950s. Company facilities included a recreation room, where the men played cards."

The children of some of the workers described how they would sneak down at night to watch their parents dance.

Several former company employees described their work as "dirty and smelly," the EPA report says, and others complained of excessive noise and dangerous conditions. Nevertheless, several said they recalled their experiences there "with fondness."

"I don't think it was so smelly," recalled former Creosote resident Donna Christopherson, daughter-in-law of a plant official.

"[Henry] Christopherson, who worked as an assistant superintendent, reported that the company donated light poles for the local high school's football field, and presented hams and turkeys to employees during the holiday season," the report says. "Delbert McDonald, another former employee, recalled that the plant had a baseball team, and that workers enjoyed a camaraderie."

Several islanders who grew up in Creosote recalled their lives there with fondness. The dangers from the chemical pollution were unknown at the time, they said, and in the summer, kids swam and fished in close proximity to the plant.

"Dad built a float for us with a diving board on it and everything," recalled Don Christopherson, son of the plant's assistant superintendent. "They used to dump the garbage off the dock there, and we used to see how many cans we could bring up from the bottom.

"We would catch crab and clams, and we wouldn't even go home for lunch. We'd build a fire on the beach, and we had an old pot there that we used to cook them in."

"We'd go shrimping right off the boom there, right next to the creosoted logs," his wife Donna said. "And here we are! We swam right down next to the Eagledale bridge, and now it's all yucky."

The plant provided jobs for many young people in the community. Reid Hansen, lifelong Crystal Springs resident, recalled working as a log peeler there in his teens. During World War II, workers were scarce, and several island residents who were in their teens at the time said the creosote plant was their first employer.

"I really enjoyed working down there in the summertime," said Don Christopherson. "I started when I was 17."

He and his wife said neither they nor most of their friends knew how to swim, but that didn't stop him from working on the massive log rafts, called "booms."

"I'll tell you a funny story about this boom guy," Donna Christopherson said. "We got in this fight, and he took off for the boom. I took out after him. But I couldn't

Eagle's-Eye View
The heart of Creosote's operations was the building with the sloping roof, upper right, that housed the massive "retorts," horizontal steam vacuum cookers that injected chemicals into logs and beams. The retorts, whose round steel doors can be seen below the roof, were among the largest in the world.

Pacific Creosoting Co. Eagle Harbor, Wn
Birds-eye View of Plant.

BIHS 4130

BIHS 4022

Waiting in Line

Logs form complex patterns in the holding ponds around the creosote plant,
waiting to be treated with chemicals for use as pilings, lumber, and timbers.

walk the boom, so he knew he was safe to get out there."

The work, however, remained difficult and dangerous. Delbert McDonald, who was employed as a bark peeler, said that even though he had been "hearing-impaired since birth, he was bothered by the loud noise of the peeling machinery," the EPA report says.

McDonald's brother Frank was injured when a log fell on his leg. The plant had no medical facilities, and Frank McDonald had to be transported to Winslow for treatment. Safety procedures were improved after the plant was unionized in 1937, according to the report.

It describes the plant as an "essential" economic force.

"Throughout the early twentieth century, the creosote plant remained a focal point for the residents of Bainbridge Island, many of whom were employed there," the report says. "During this period, it was essential to the local economy as well as to that of the region, becoming one of the largest wood preserving facilities in the world."

Products were sold all over the world.

"One former employee reported seeing treated pilings from the plant in Camh Ranh Bay, Vietnam, in 1969-70," the report says. "So important was the plant to the national defense effort that some employees were exempted from the draft."

When the plant was bought by the Baxter-Wyckoff Company in 1959, however, it was a pollution-soaked bomb waiting for environmental watchdogs to light the fuse. For more than half a century, the earth around the plant had been flooded with petroleum products, heavy metals, and other toxic chemicals.

The treatment that had proved so effective against wood-borers was killing fish, shellfish, and their habitat in large parts of Eagle Harbor and surrounding waters.

In the 1980s, the EPA called the area one of the most toxic in the nation and placed it on the agency's Superfund list for an intensive cleanup. The company that operated Creosote and the Seattle plant declared bankruptcy.

The EPA removed the structures on the site and began to remove the toxic materials. One official estimated that the process could take fifty years or more and cost millions of dollars.

Residents urged the government to make the site a park.

View of Eagle Harbor, Wn. and plant of Pacific Creosoting Co.

BIHS 4129

Walk to Work

Pacific Creosote's plant was built over water, making it closer to its log supply. Workers had only a short walk to work from company-supplied housing. Tenants in the 1940s included Bill Brisbois, sea captain; Henry Christopherson, assistant plant superintendent; John Nelson; Charlie Lane; Christy Beam; Art Paynter; John Sennet, fire chief; Oscar Anderson; Clyde McDonald; and Bob Bell.

Creosote's General Store

The company store had a good location, both view-wise and dock-wise. Cynthia Sennett, mother of longtime Bainbridge Fire Chief John Sennett, ran the store.

BIHS 4126

Rockaway Getaway

BIHS 2213

Rockaway Beach wasn't quite the attraction in the early 1900s that it is today. Residents complained of strong winds, dangerous tides, and lack of sunshine past noon. Fishermen and squatters built shacks there. Note the size of the driftwood stump, far left. The beach became prime property later.

BIHS1188

Rockaway Shipyard

The Hall brothers weren't Bainbridge Island's only shipbuilders. The Moran brothers built ships in the 1880s on Rockaway Beach. After the Alaska gold rush began in 1889, they built steamers for mining companies, launching them sideways at high tide. "In all, twelve specially designed riverboats were built here and in Seattle, and they became the backbone of the Yukon fleet," historian Katy Warner says in a note attached to the back of this photograph.

Putt 'er There
*Pebble Beach would be hard-pressed to match the spectacular setting of the
Country Club golf course on Restoration Point. It was built between 1896 and 1915.*

Chapter Eighteen

Country Club

The southeast jut of Bainbridge Island, called Restoration Point, may truly be classed as historic, for that famous Englishman, Captain George Vancouver, discoverer of Puget Sound, in the Spring of 1792, brought his two vessels, the sloop, **Discovery,** *and tender,* **Chatham,** *to anchor in the lee of this point.*

—T. M. Pelly

Captain George Vancouver waded ashore about noon on May 20, 1792, to meet the first residents of Bainbridge Island. It was a gorgeous spring day, and he apparently enjoyed the social occasion with his hosts and the spectacular view from the promontory.

He named it Village Point. But then the explorer changed his mind.

"This name he later changed to 'Restoration Point' owing to his having celebrated Restoration Day (the anniversary of the return of the Stuarts to the English throne) *'whilst at anchor under it,'*" writes Tom Pelly in *The Story of Restoration Point and the Country Club.*

The island's inhabitants had called the point simply "camping area." The point got another new name from Lieutenant Charles Wilkes when he charted Bainbridge waters in 1841.

"Wilkes renamed Restoration Point 'Gordon Point' in honor of one of his quartermasters but, as in most cases of this nature, the original geo-

Elizabeth and Alexander Fisken

The Light on Blakely Rock
In the early twentieth century, Blakely Rock just north of Restoration Point was larger than it was at the end of the millennium. Old-timers recall rowing out to it for picnics, fishing, and climbs up the light post. Fishermen also gathered kelp there.

graphical name has survived."

Pelly's book, which includes an addendum written by G. C. Nickum, provides the most complete record of any community on the island and probably in Kitsap County as well. Pelly covers the Country Club of Seattle from 1891 through 1931. Nickum extends Pelly's narrative on to 1984.

Pelly's father was a founding member of the Country Club, and young Pelly lived in his father's house off and on when he wasn't in Olympia or Washington, D.C.

The younger Pelly had been president of Lowman and Hanford, an early Seattle publishing company specializing in local history, before being elected to the state legislature.

In 1952, he was elected to the U.S. House of Representatives. He "was once one of the best booksellers in Seattle," wrote Nard Jones, a *Seattle Post-Intelligencer* editor, in his book, *Seattle,* published in 1972.

Pelly was a thorough historian. The U.S. sloop-of-war *Decatur,* sent to protect Seattle residents in the Indian War of 1855-1856, went aground on the reef of Restoration Point. The ship got off the reef and was repaired "in time or else the history of Seattle and the Northwest would be a less happy and quite different story," he writes.

During the 1850s, the Country Club area was known as "Bean's

Built to Last

The Country Club's members built a sturdy clubhouse on Restoration Point with space for parties. It was still in use a century later.

BIHS Historic Properties 18-1

some sort.

"The first of these was the *Roxie,* a cutter about thirty feet in length, chartered in 1886 by E. A. Strout and G. H. Heilbron. These two and their friends would go off for weekends and vacations about Puget Sound, and it was in the *Roxie* that the founders of the Country Club 'discovered' Restoration Point."

The men foresaw the need for a retreat from Seattle's urbanization. In 1888, they "conceived the idea of obtaining some land . . . where they could erect a cabin of some sort for spending the night."

They decided to buy the tip of Restoration Point. But the plan was postponed by calamity. Seattle burned down in 1889, causing a depression.

Nevertheless, "on April 16, 1891, for the sum of $1,010, the five and a half acres" on the point were purchased from Gus Sanders. Then they talked Gus into building them a clubhouse on the tip of the point. It has survived for more than a century "in practically the same manner as it stands today except that it was partitioned into two bunkrooms at the S.E. end (the Mount Rainier side)," Pelly says.

"The fireplace instead of being at the side, where it is now, was in the center and was built back into the bunkrooms," he writes. "Josiah Collins had a theory that a chimney was unnecessary, that a small opening in the roof would be sufficient. This 'siwash' chimney lasted only a short time, and before it was changed the members and their guests breathed a great deal of smoke."

The first official meeting of the club's fifteen charter members was held May 16, 1891. But social activities didn't begin until the following summer. As the members' families expanded, so did the club's property. They bought Gus Sanders out, then sold his farm back to him when times got tough, and then bought it back in 1903.

The tiny bunkhouse got crowded, and the men needed room for

Point," named for Reuben Bean, who had a claim west of the point where Fort Ward was built. He was killed, perhaps by native residents, in 1859, Pelly writes.

The Country Club property's first owner was Theodore O. Williams, former sheriff of Kitsap County. He sold his land to a man named Erick Gustave "Gus" Sanders in 1868 for $200.

But the Country Club wasn't born until 1888 when several young Seattle boating enthusiasts saw the point and its protected anchorage as an inviting spot to spend summer weekends.

"Out of the heterogeneous 'many' who came to the growing town of Seattle during the 'eighties' were a few younger men who formed an unusually congenial clique," Pelly writes. "These men were drawn together by many ties, not the least of which was their mutual fondness for sports. Sailing was a favorite recreation, and various members of this group, together or individually, rarely were without a boat of families. Several built cabins, which were enlarged over the years until they became magnificent mansions. They added tennis courts, a swimming pool, and stables for the many horses they owned.

And they built "the first golf course in the vicinity of Seattle," according to Pelly. The story is worth repeating.

> J. Gillison, of Tacoma, was an intimate friend of the members and a frequent visitor at the Club. Returning from a trip to Scotland in 1896 he brought back with him some odd-shaped sticks and gutta per-cha balls which he presented to the Club. Two tin cans were sunk in the ground on what is now our second fairway and thus was the beginning of golf on our shores. . . .
>
> The first tournament was held June 20, 1896, the course being played twice, and the winner was Harry Meserve with a score of twenty-five for the four holes. A second competition was held in August, won jointly by E. A. Strout and W. A. Peters, each turning in cards of nineteen.

Later that year, the course was enlarged to six holes, and, in another tournament, the contestants played the holes three times. The

BIHS Historic Properties 18-4

The William McEwan House
The William McEwans built this house, designed by Carl Gould, on lot four of the club in 1915. Gould also designed the home of McEwan's brother, Alexander, on lot two to the west, which was in continuous family ownership into the twenty-first century.

winners scored ninety-eight. Three more holes were added in 1915.

The club's first forty years were "a period of rapid growth followed by years of stability," Nickum reports. Members moved from a bunkhouse to separate cottages, then permanent homes. At the beginning of the twenty-first century, most of the homes were still owned by members' descendants.

"During the first 40 years of the Club's life, over 40 different individuals owned membership in the Club," he says. "Since 1931, however, only nine members have resigned and been replaced by new members outside of the Country Club families."

Room to Play
Riding was a major club pastime, and "practically every family had at least one horse and most of them had two or more." The dock, right, was used by steamboats to provide transportation to and from Seattle.

Elizabeth and Alexander Fisken

Fort Ward at Bean Point

This picture of the Army post at Bean Point was taken at 11:30 a.m. June 28, 1932. Nine years later, antisubmarine netting, upper right, was stretched across Rich Passage to Manchester to protect the Bremerton Navy Yard from enemy submarines. The U.S. Navy took over the fort during World War II for a radio school and top-secret listening post to intercept Japanese code messages.

Chapter Nineteen

Fort Ward

In its teens, Fort Ward guarded the approaches to Bremerton Naval Shipyard. At 35 or so, it was a summer camp for children. But in its forties, the obscure fort on Bainbridge Island was given a new job—listening to the enemy.

Ivan W. Lee Jr. profiles the military facility in his book, *The Story of the Little Fort at Bean Point,* a remarkably detailed history both of the fort and of early-day military life.

"Fort Ward was one of several Coast Artillery forts built from about 1885 to 1915 in a period of modernization of our military facilities," he writes. "Built to fight the classic wars by land and sea, it became obsolete upon the advent of effective aircraft."

Lee, a ham radio operator, became intrigued by the fort's role as a secret listening post in World War II after his daughter, Sarah, bought the building where radio operators wrote down Japanese messages and sent them to Washington, D.C.

The fort had its beginnings in 1890, two and a half months after Washington became a state. On January 23, the new legislature granted the U.S. Army permission "to purchase the land as wanted for fortifications, lighthouses, or other needed public buildings."

BIHS 1681

Practicing for War

Fort Ward was an important training site in both world wars. Here, soldiers practice sighting wheel-mounted heavy machine guns on bivouac during World War I.

The Army bought 750 acres that included land on Bainbridge Island's Bean Point and across Rich Passage on Middle Point, which later became Manchester. The fort and three others like it on Admiralty Inlet were needed to protect the new shipyard the Navy planned to build in Bremerton.

The Army built two forts at the mouth of Admiralty Inlet northeast of the Quimper Peninsula. One was Fort Worden north of the town of Port Townsend. The second was Fort Flagler on the northern tip of Marrowstone Island across the bay from the town.

The third, Fort Casey, was built across Admiralty Inlet on Whidbey Island.

The three forts were the Army's main coastal defense. Fort Ward was supposed to provide last-chance protection for Bremerton.

But in the beginning, the Army had grander plans for Rich Passage's defenses.

"The original scheme was to have a large number of fortifications, most of them at Middle Point," Lee says. "They would include heavy 'disappearing' guns and a battery of 12-inch seacoast mortars. Under this plan, the mine facilities would also be located at Middle Point."

Battery Nash

Before World War I, Fort Ward was equipped with huge mounted artillery pieces to protect the Bremerton shipyard from enemy ships. Battery Nash, the largest of four gun emplacements at the fort, was built between 1900 and 1903, and was equipped with three eight-inch rifled guns installed on carriages that swiveled the guns out of sight for crews to reload them. The guns never fired a shell in anger.

The fort on Bean Point would protect the mine field with smaller guns along Rich Passage. Bean Point was going to be a sub-post of Middle Point. But the Army changed its mind after construction had begun.

"The big-gun defenses would be at Forts Worden, Flagler, and Casey," Lee writes. "Fort Ward's mission would be only to support the mine field."

The fort's administrative facilities and living quarters for the men would be on Bean Point. Construction began just before the Spanish-American war in 1898, and the facility was mineless when war was declared in April of that year.

The Army considered using dynamite-filled beer kegs to defend Bremerton if necessary, but the three-month war was over before the plan could be carried out.

The Army Corps of Engineers turned the completed Middle Point facilities over to the Coast Artillery Corps on December 4, 1905, but the Army shut them down five years later, "as soon as mine facilities were duplicated at Bean Point," Lee says.

The War Department gave the Middle Point facility to the Navy during World War I for oil storage, and the area was called Manchester.

In 1903, Fort Ward's artillery batteries were completed. Battery Nash, which was the southern- and eastern-most installation guarding the entrance to Rich Passage, was the largest, with three eight-inch guns. (Eight-inch means the projectile the gun fired is eight inches in diameter.) Battery Warner below it had two rapid-fire five-inch guns.

Farther west toward Port Orchard were Battery Vinton with three three-inch guns and Battery Thornburg with four three-inch guns.

The fort was designed to house a "company" of men, which in those days numbered about a hundred. The base's official roster for 1914 lists the base commander, two lieutenants, ten sergeants, twelve corporals, eighty-eight privates, and six cooks, mechanics, and musicians for a total of one hundred nineteen.

The post exchange-gymnasium, 104, also of brick construction but only one story plus basement, was a very important part of the fort's "social life." The east half was used for activities requiring a high ceiling. At that end the brickwork was a little better, and the flooring was narrower and more carefully selected. The ceiling, right up on the rafters, was about the same quality as the flooring and beautifully varnished.

The west half, or slightly more, was devoted to the post exchange. There had been so many later alterations that its arrangement is not clear, but it probably provided space for tables for cards and other games, and maybe simply visiting.

The full basement provided space for a bowling alley, weight-lifting, and probably other activities, as well as showers.

Planning to stay permanently, the Army built most of the fort's seventeen buildings out of brick.

At the beginning of World War I, the Army and Navy were short of artillery. So the Army shipped Battery Nash's guns to the war zone.

Most of the fort's smaller guns were removed in 1920 except for the two five-inch guns at Battery Warner below Battery Nash. The government removed those in the 1950s.

The Army officially abandoned Fort Ward as a Coast Artillery Station March 12, 1928, but retained ownership of the property. A two-man security detail guarded the site until 1933.

"For a time the facilities were used by the Washington State Department of Public Welfare, which assisted almost 1,000 girls and boys of families that were on State relief rolls," Lee writes. "They were given good food and opportunities to enjoy the 375-acre wooded area and the beautiful beach.

"There was some discussion of turning the facilities into a home for unemployed men. Such a proposal definitely did not find favor in the South Bainbridge community."

In 1938, the Navy acquired the property for a recreation site. Then in 1941, with war imminent, the post's activities increased significantly. One of the first island families to feel the war preparations was the Petersons of Sunny Hill Dairy north of the fort. Lee tells their story:

On a spring morning of 1941, 10-year-old Dorothy answered a knock at the door. The visitor was certainly not a neighbor—he was wearing riding boots and a hat—and he wanted to talk to her father.

When the stranger left, her father, William Peterson, looked 10 years older. The man had told him the Navy wanted their property. They would be paid $9,000—much less than the worth of a successful small dairy farm of very good reputation. They would have to remove all their cows and other livestock, but leave everything else except their personal possessions. They were to remove no plants, because the Navy wanted it to look like someone was living there.

And the family had less than 30 days to get out. Moving the dairy on such short notice, much less sell the cows for a fair price, was out of

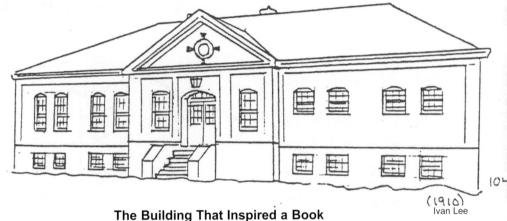

The Building That Inspired a Book

Fort Ward's important role in World War II might never have been recorded if Ivan and Lois Lee's daughter Sarah hadn't bought the fort's former post exchange building in 1985. Ivan Lee, a ham radio operator and Boeing engineer, became fascinated with the building's use as a top-secret listening post and, with his wife's and daughter's help, wrote The Story of the Little Fort at Bean Point, *published in 1993 after his death.*

the question. William, at age 45, would have to find a new job to support his wife, Edith, and their two young daughters.

The Petersons were able to sell most of their livestock. They moved to West Seattle, where William Peterson found work in a shipyard.

"After having told the Petersons that the farm would be preserved as-is, the Navy 'torched' everything—the barn and other outbuildings, except the house itself. . . . The house was remodeled to become a two-family officers' quarters," Lee writes. The Petersons stood on the beach at West Seattle and watched the smoke rise from the fire."

BIHS 3699

Parade Ground

To keep in shape, Fort Ward's peacetime soldiers played lots of baseball on the ballfield in front of the impressive brick enlisted men's barracks, built around 1910. After this photo was taken about 1916, the Army painted the fort's name in large letters on the roof to guide airplane pilots.

The Navy also seized two other farms in the area, adding 120 acres to the base, and it built a tall wire-mesh fence around the area.

One dispossessed property owner committed suicide. A relative of Chief Seattle, Annie Dahlstrom, who lived in the woods near the Petersons, lost access to the outside world because the fence cut her off from the Petersons' road. Lee says Dahlstrom had to hoist her deceased husband's red flannel underwear up a flagpole as a signal that she needed to be rescued.

But the fort was preparing for an important mission in the war. It was to become a Naval Receiving Station, listening to Japanese coded messages. The Navy built two tall antenna systems, one at the fort for listening and another at Battle Point eight miles away for talking.

"The transmitter was located so far away for good reason," Lee writes. "Listening was a 24-hour-a-day task at the NRS. A high-powered transmitter close to the receiving antennas would have caused intolerable interference."

The post masqueraded as a radio training school. But the school's graduates were put to work intercepting messages from Japan to its military commanders and diplomats. The listeners copied the messages and sent them by teletype to Washington, D.C., for decoding.

To find qualified listeners, the Navy turned in part to amateur radio enthusiasts, known as "hams." After Pearl Harbor, they volunteered in droves.

"The hams of those years were highly motivated," Lee writes. "They learned by self-study and by doing; they had 'hands-on' experience in operating—including Morse code—and a working knowledge of antennas and the insides of radio transmitters and receivers. The military was able to put most hams to work after very little specialized training."

Six months after Pearl Harbor, "15,000 out of 50,000 hams were in uniform," Lee says.

Among those who underwent training at Fort Ward were Jack Klamm and Vince Wolf, who became permanent island residents. Klamm had earned a ham license in 1933 while still in high school.

"He also contributed to what we know about the day-to-day operation of the early Naval Radio Station," Lee says.

"Late in March, twenty eager, green-as-grass Naval Reservists" became the fort's Class Number 2, Klamm writes in a chapter for Lee's book. Because he and another recruit already had ham licenses, they were promoted to Seaman First Class. Klamm says he taught some of the "bonehead" classes for recruits who had difficulty with the course.

The recruits were warned not to discuss the base with outsiders.

"We were forbidden to even go near the radio station building, even though we had to pass right in front of it on our way to the mess hall in the big wooden building to the east," Klamm says.

"Officially we were not even to acknowledge that anything but an

Battle Point's Towers

Jack Klamm

The tall antennas at Battle Point Park were transmitting towers, not receivers. Antennas at Fort Ward did the receiving. The transmitters had to be built several miles away from the receivers to eliminate interference.

ordinary radio school existed at the fort."

Klamm graduated first in his class in July and was assigned to the Navy radio station in Bremerton.

On December 2, 1941, five days before the Japanese bombed Pearl Harbor, Bremerton radiomen "became painfully aware that a number of Japanese naval radio stations had shifted their operating frequencies to exactly the same as key United States Naval frequencies in the Pacific area," Klamm says.

The Japanese had used similar jamming tactics in the past to disrupt enemy communications prior to a military action. The chief in charge of the station ordered it put on wartime alert status "without waiting for orders he never did get," Klamm says. "The jamming ceased on Saturday, Dec. 6th."

Early Sunday morning, Fort Ward's listeners intercepted a broadcast from Japan to the country's ambassador in Washington, D.C., ordering him to break off peace talks. They didn't hear the message from Hawaii telling of the attack several hours later.

"They were listening to Japanese radio frequencies," Lee writes. "The news actually arrived on the teletype. Rumor has it that the operator immediately typed out a duplicate for the station files and pocketed the original."

The attack at 8 a.m. Hawaii time—11 a.m. on the West Coast and 2 p.m. in Washington, D.C.—caused turmoil at bases everywhere.

"At the Naval Shipyard, sailors reported aboard in droves," Klamm says. "The first hundred or so, still in their dress blue uniforms, were herded aboard buses bound for Manchester—the old Middle Point sub-post of Fort Ward, now in Navy custody. They were pressed into service completing the submarine nets that were in the process of being fabricated for installation across Rich Passage to protect the Bremerton Navy Yard."

They got little to eat, and, on the third day, began returning to the shipyard, "tired beyond belief, dirtier than they had ever been, hands bloody from the rough steel cables and cable clamps and with their uniforms in rags, but their heads up because the nets were being put in place," Klamm says.

The Bremerton shipyard's new enemy in World War II was submarines, not surface ships. Heavy nets with explosives attached were installed across Rich and Agate Passages, and Fort Ward personnel guarded and maintained them.

Former radiomen told Lee the fort was one of the first Navy installations to receive female enlistees, known as WAVES. Their presence improved morale and forced the sloppily dressed radiomen to clean up their appearance.

Fort Ward's listening activities didn't end with World War II. With the beginning of the Cold War, the radio operators had a new set of

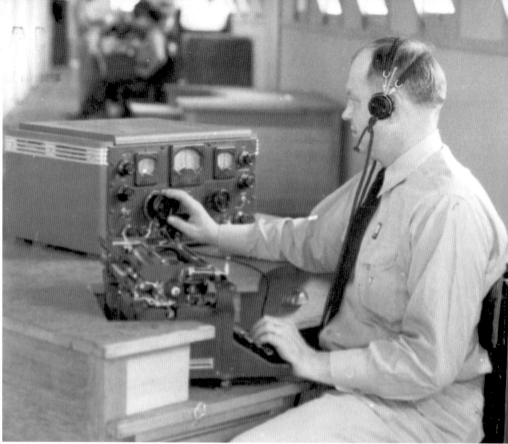

BIHS 1631

Even the Room Was Classified
Chief Radioman Hess adjusts his shortwave radio receiver in a picture probably taken in 1943. The print is stamped CONFIDENTIAL.

transmitters to listen to, made in the Soviet Union. And the weapons the Army used for defending Bremerton became more lethal.

During the war, rapid-fire anti-aircraft guns had guarded Puget Sound's military installations. Afterwards, they were replaced by guided missiles.

"The final chapter of the Fort Ward military history involved an even newer generation of anti-aircraft artillery," Lee writes. "Fort Ward's final role was minor and brief, and like the first one, might have been significant, but turned out not to be. However, the association with the 'new artillery' permitted the old fort to go out of business on the leading edge of technology, if only for a couple of years."

In the early 1950s, the 513th Anti-Aircraft Artillery Battalion

Inside Peek at a Top-Secret Listening Post

Tall radio towers at Battle Point and Fort Ward helped defeat Japan in World War II. The Fort Ward tower captured coded messages from Japanese ships and land stations, and copies were transmitted via Battle Point to Washington, D.C., for deciphering. Japan didn't learn until after the war that the United States had broken its codes.

moved in at the fort, overseeing four Nike guided-missile batteries.

One was located at Strawberry Hill Park on Bainbridge Island. To guide the missiles, the Army set up a radar antenna on Ward Avenue in Eagledale. Other batteries were in Kingston, Poulsbo, and Olalla.

Toward the end of the decade, the Army installed more powerful missiles called Nike Ajax.

"To administer this refurbishment at Winslow, the headquarters staff of the 513th AAA Battalion was moved to Fort Ward from Manchester," Lee says. "The Navy was closing out its radio station, and the Army and Navy coexisted for a little while."

Where did they store these missiles? In the basement of the build-

ing Lee's daughter would purchase thirty years later and convert into a residence.

Fort Ward's last military tenant left in July 1958. The government sold the part of the fort along the waterfront to the state for a park. The rest went to private purchasers. Most of the brick buildings remained.

The First Generation
Zenhichi Harui, left, his nephew Kaichi Seko, third from left, and two friends used a gasoline-powered saw built by Harui to cut old-growth firs on land in Island Center for a commercial garden that has been in the family more than ninety years. Harui and his brother, Zenmatsu Seko, came to Bainbridge Island in the early 1900s.

Chapter Twenty

Our Ethnic Communities

We are a melting pot. Swedes. Chinese. Norwegians. Croatians. Japanese. Filipinos. Native Americans. Finns, Irish, Scots, Brits, Germans, French, Spaniards, Portuguese.

Many were part of the largest mass movement in history. They came by boat and wagon train, looking for work or for cheap land. Many Norwegians congregated on the north end of the island. The Japanese who came to work at Port Blakely built houses on the hill south of the mill and sent for their wives. Chinese men who cooked at the Port Madison mill and hotel lived on the Sandspit.

Many of this island's first residents were American-born, mostly from New England. People from other countries sold their possessions for enough money to buy a boat ticket. All were trying to grab a part of the American Dream.

The sawmills established at Port Madison and Port Blakely were voracious consumers of people. They needed loggers and roustabouts. The mills did a lively trade with countries around the Pacific, and their ships gave cheap transport to potential recruits.

"Many of these different people were only here a short time," says the Minority History Committee of the Bainbridge Island School District in *They Cast a Long Shadow*. "These were the Chinese,

BIHS 117

Jitsuzo and Shima Nakata
The Nakatas founded a dynasty that by the end of the century numbered nearly 100 persons influential in the community.

Hawaiians, and some Japanese and Filipinos who came here to work at the biggest sawmill in the world. They could earn money here that they couldn't earn in their homes far away. Here they lived in their own little villages for a few years, working hard and saving what they could. When they had enough saved up, they went back home to live with their families."

But many stayed.

"They liked this country and found enough friendly people here to make them feel welcome," the history says. "These people were mostly Filipinos and Japanese. They worked hard too, and started families here. They became Americans. Their children, grandchildren, and great-grandchildren are Americans too."

Some workers had been here all along. Suquamish tribal members worked at Meigs's sawmill and sold fish and shellfish to the mill's cookhouse.

In the early years, Bainbridge Island's Asian population remained small. The 1857 Slaughter County census lists twenty-one aliens among its 169 residents, not one of whom was from Asia. *They Cast a Long Shadow* says a census taken in 1883 "showed about twenty Chinese men who lived at Port Madison. They worked as laundrymen, fishermen, and cooks."

"Some of the Chinese men were listed in the census by their real names, but others were only given nicknames," the book says, such as "China Charlie" and "Old Sam."

"The census taker found two Japanese men at Port Madison. He listed them as 'Japan Joe' and 'Charles Jose.' Either he didn't bother to get their names right, or they didn't know enough English to make him understand."

The official found "dozens of Chinese" at Port Blakely.

"Finally he stopped asking for their names or even their nicknames," the book says. "On the last page of his list, he just wrote 'Chinaman' 39 times."

Fredi Perry in her book, *Port Madison, Washington Territory,* said the territorial census in 1889 showed 261 residents in Port Madison; two were Chinese, both cooks.

Bainbridge Island didn't experience the violence against Chinese immigrants that swept Seattle, Tacoma, and other cities. But in December 1875, G. W. Bullene, superintendent of the Port Madison mill, discharged all of the Chinese workers. They went elsewhere, to be replaced by other workers from Asia and South America.

The Japanese had greater incentive to stay. Jobs were scarce back home.

"Many young men arrived from Japan with only one suit, a bedroll, and less than $10 to their name and no passport," the Minority History Committee says. "No questions were asked about the passport. They could go to work at the mill right away for $1.30 or $1.40 a day. They also got meals and a place to sleep."

The men had little to do besides working, gambling, "and sometimes acting rowdy." said Kihachi Hirakawa, who came to work at the mill in 1890 and wrote about it:

In the camp of the sawmill there were 24 Japanese living together at the same place. . . . They were working 10 hours every day except Sunday, but every night were gambling until midnight or 2 or 3 o'clock in the morning. . . . I couldn't sleep by their noisy talk or sometimes (they would) quarrel or fight.

About a year later, a Mr. Fujita of the Japanese Consulate visited Port Blakely to see how the Japanese were doing. He looked in at the bunkhouse at 10 o'clock in the morning. He was shocked. Thirty men

BIHS 426

Taking a Break
Gooley, left, Port Madison Hotel's wash man, relaxes on the hotel's deck while Sam Wing-kie, the cook, reads a scroll.

were in there, gambling when they should have been working.

Mr. Fujita wrote an angry report back to his consulate. He told them there were 80 Japanese at the mill, but only twelve of those were "honest workers." Another fifty worked only when they needed the money. The rest were full time gamblers.

Not only that, but some of the gamblers were free loaders. "Pretending they were employed," he said, "they ate with the men in the dining room and spent the rest of the time doing nothing but gambling. No condemning remarks will indeed be too harsh to describe the shameless conduct of these Japanese."

Hanjiro Kono, boss of the Japanese mill workers, stopped the gambling in 1894, and many of the men left. They were replaced by "good, earnest farmers" looking for a permanent home.

"The mill company set aside some land where the new families could live without paying rent," the minority history says. ". . . [T]he company gave the families lumber to build themselves a village."

The Japanese called it Nagaya. The whites called it Japtown. The town was in a ravine above Port Blakely's south shore. As the

Wedding Day

Charlie "Chinaman," Port Madison's cookhouse steward, poses for a picture with his new bride.

BIHS 1038

Japanese population grew, the town expanded up the hill, and a new village was created called Yama.

Other ethnic groups had communities nearby, the Minority Historty Committee report says. Hawaiian workers built a village next to Nagaya and Yama.

"There were also Spanish, Italian, Swedish, and Finnish neighborhoods," the report says.

Then there was Toe Jam Hill. How it got its name is still in dispute.

"On Toejam Hill there was a colony of people from several different nations," the committee report says. "These people spent a lot of time in the tavern at the foot of the hill. When the bartender saw them coming, he would say, 'I'll just mix up a little toejam for them. By 'toejam' he meant any old rotgut he could find on the shelves. So the place was called Toejam Hill."

Bainbridge Review columnist Katy Warner tells a different story.

"To my way of thinking the most colorful name of any neighborhood here is that of the community up on the hill, above John Graham's home, on the Country Club Road," she writes in a column published November 22, 1961. "Sometimes it is referred to as Port Blakely Heights, but its cor-

Nagaya

Japanese immigrants built their own town around 1900 in a ravine south of Port Blakely. They called it Nagaya. The European immigrants called it Japtown. The two-story Washington Hotel, built by Hanjiro Kono and later run by Sohichi Shigemura, is on the left. The bridge in the foreground spanned the ravine that split the community. As more Japanese arrived, they built homes above Nagaya, calling the new settlement Yama.

rect name is Torjam Hill, although the old timers often called it Toyem, Trojan or Toejam Hill."

Warner says Jorgen Hansen, who lived there, told her its first resident was named Torjam.

"Apparently he was a very popular fellow and well liked," she says. "He made many friends in the mill and they often visited him. When planning a visit, one fellow would say to another, 'Let's go to Torjam's Hill."

But the nickname stuck and Torjam was forgotten, Warner says.

By 1903, the Japanese towns had three hundred residents, three bathhouses, two barbershops, and two churches.

Mill boss Hanjiro Kono built a hotel in the village with ten guest rooms and a restaurant that served Japanese noodles.

Kiyonosuke Takayoshi, a former soldier known as General Takayoshi, started a store and ice cream parlor, which drew customers from all over the island. He also had a photo studio, watch repair business, and dance hall, and raised chickens, pigs, and cows.

The houses in Yama and Nagaya didn't have running water. The women carried water from the creek for bathing and washing clothes. Many of the Japanese women also worked as housekeepers. Torazo and Kuma Nakao settled in Yama, which means "mountain" in Japanese. Torazo became known as Slab Harry because he collected the useless outer slabs of wood from the logs that the mill normally burned and sold them to Mosquito Fleet boats for fuel. Kuma Nakao walked to Crystal Springs to clean houses, earning fifty cents a day.

"It was fun to live in Port Blakely," said their son Sam, who was born in 1914. "Everyone in the town knew everyone else. People had

Keeping Traditions Alive

BIHS 637

Two children pose in traditional kimono at the Japanese American Community's annual picnic sometime in the late 1920s or early 1930s.

come from all over the world to work at the mill. Even though they lived in clusters according to place of origin, there was little discrimination. The town was most democratic."

The Port Blakely mill closed in 1922, and the buildings were dismantled in 1924. A year later, Nagaya and Yama burned down.

Among the Nakaos' neighbors were the Nakatas. Torazo Nakao

The Second Wave

Eddie Corpuz, left, his brothers Evaristo and Miguel, and cousin Anacleto were still school boys when they came in the second wave of immigrants from the Philippine Islands between 1906 and 1934. Many of them worked in Alaska's canneries during the fishing season.

Filipino American Community

and Jitsuzo Nakata were from the same prefecture in Japan, and they and their families became lifelong friends. They were also instrumental with several other Japanese pioneers in helping to develop Bainbridge Island's strawberry industry.

Another pioneer was Yasuji Suyematsu, who had a farm on the old territorial road south of Port Madison where Day Road was later built. His son Akio continued the family farming tradition, growing strawberries, Christmas trees, and pumpkins into the twenty-first century.

"The soil and weather on Bainbridge Island are just right for strawberries," the minority history says. "One of the the island's first Japanese farmers, Shinichi Moritani, proved it. He grew the island's

first strawberries in 1908. The next year six more Japanese farmers planted strawberries. Theirs did well too. 'All you needed to grow strawberries,' said one farmer, 'was one horse, one plow, and lots of kids.'"

Strawberry planting, picking, and marketing were community-wide activities.

"The fruit was canned in the home of Sakakichi Sumiyoshi, one of the growers," the minority committee says. "Everybody got together to do that."

In 1917 when the job outgrew the Sumiyoshi kitchen, farmers shipped their crop to a Seattle cannery. Island strawberries became famous.

In the 1920s, the farmers built a cannery on Eagle Harbor. The plant workers were from families all over the island, not just from the Japanese community.

The strawberry fields lured two other ethnic communities to the island—Filipinos and Canadian Indians. C. Tobby Membrere, a Filipino, landed in Seattle on May 31, 1928, with twenty-five dollars in his pocket.

"My first job was in Tacoma on a poultry farm," he said in Phoebe Smith's *Glimpses of Bainbridge*. "I earned forty dollars a month and board and room. We worked from dawn to dark and had one day a month off. It was a tough job.

"The following June, I came to Bainbridge Island because I heard strawberry pickers were needed. I met Philip Morales and Nick Bucsit. They were good people and became good friends. I think they were the first Filipinos to come here in 1927, though there were some who came earlier during the Port Blakely days."

Membrere picked strawberries for the Nakatas and worked in Alaskan fish canneries. After 1929, jobs became scarce everywhere, and Membrere and others became seasonal pickers, following the crops from California to Canada.

During Bainbridge Island's frenetic strawberry picking and packing season, Canadian Indians came to the island to work. Many married Filipinos and remained on the island.

"Every able-bodied person in an Indian family would come to pick strawberries," the minority history says. "There were no babysitters or day care centers for the babies. The Indian mothers had to take care of their children and pick too."

By 1940, much of the land between Winslow and Island Center had been cleared and planted with strawberries. Most of the land was bought in the names of the children of first-generation Japanese because the state constitution prohibited aliens from owning land unless they could become citizens. The Japanese couldn't become citizens because a federal law denied citizenship for Asians.

When the Imperial Japanese Navy bombed U.S. military bases in Hawaii on December 7, 1941, fear, panic, and prejudice tore the fabric of island communities asunder. Men and women who had spent most of their adult lives on the island were suddenly suspected as enemies. Their children, American citizens by birth, were shunned. Here's what the minority history has to say about those perilous times:

The U.S. government knew [the Japanese residents] were loyal. But the country turned against them anyway. Rumors began to spread. There was a rumor that the Japanese farmers planted their strawberries in rows that pointed to Bremerton. That was supposed to guide airplanes from Japan to the Navy Yard, so they could bomb it.

There was another story that the farmers had dynamite. People said they would use it to blow up the Navy Yard, Fort Ward, and the Battle Point radio station. The FBI checked out the stories. Sure enough, some of the farmers did have dynamite. They used it to clear stumps. There was nothing wrong in that, but people were jittery and were afraid they might use it for evil purposes.

Frank Kitamoto had a lot of dynamite in his shed. It belonged to him and Felix Narte, his Filipino partner. They were clearing land they rented to plant more strawberries.

Filipino American Community

Always the Cooks
*The caption in the Filipino American Community's collection reads: "FILIPINO MEN—Then and now, in the Alaska canneries, the Navy, the White House. **ALWAYS THE COOKS. WHY NOT THE CANNERY OWNER, THE SHIPS CAPTAIN, THE UNITED STATES PRESIDENT?**"*

Narte spoke up for his partner, but suspicion remained. The FBI confiscated dynamite, cameras, guns, and short-wave radios belonging to Japanese families. On February 20, 1942, President Franklin D. Roosevelt "signed Executive Order 9066, which authorized the army to establish military areas from which any civilian could be excluded and to provide these 'evacuees' with transportation and other assis-

Sorting 'em Out

The Japanese American and Filipino American communities created a major new industry on the island between the world wars that helped support many island families. Japanese and Filipino farmers raised the berries, and, at harvest, high school kids and house- wives helped pick and pack them. These women are sorting berries in the old Strawberry Factory at the head of Eagle Harbor. The berries were a prized delicacy and were served to England's King George VI and Queen Elizabeth during a visit to Vancouver, B.C., in 1939. The royal entourage ordered 800 crates.

tance," writes Greg Robertson in *By Order of the President: FDR and the Internment of Japanese Americans*. "Although the text of Executive Order 9066 did not specifically mention Japanese Americans, it was intended to apply to them exclusively."

When the order was posted March 21, 1942, it gave the Japanese families eight days to pack what belongings they could and dispose of the rest. Those on Bainbridge Island were the first to go.

The families sold what they could. Soldiers using Army trucks hauled furniture and other belongings to the Japanese Community Center in Winslow where it was locked up. Three retired sea captains were appointed deputy sheriffs with the job of guarding the hall.

"There isn't any use saying anything about the evacuation," said Paul Ohtaki, a second-generation Japanese American born on the island. "It's something that is happening and we might as well make the best of it."

Ohtaki was working as a "printer's devil" for Walt and Milly Woodward, owners of the *Bainbridge Review,* when the order came down. The Woodwards took a fearless stand in support of their Japanese friends and criticized the government's action in print for the duration of the war. Walt, the paper's editor, made Ohtaki a correspon- dent, and the paper ran Ohtaki's columns about life at the camps, Manzanar and Minidoka. The *Review* was the only paper in the nation that opposed the relocation.

"About half of the Bainbridge Islanders are in favor of moving them," Walt Woodward wrote. "In fact, some say they are glad and that they hope they never come home. The other half are sorry for them and feel that they can be trusted."

Some merchants canceled their ads in the *Review.* Many readers canceled their subscriptions. The Woodwards stuck to their guns.

The minority history report tells what happened on the eighth day:

In the early morning of March 29, 1942, fifteen army trucks fanned

growled and snapped at them. Mrs. Moji tearfully led King back into the house. He had to watch through the window while his masters were taken away.

The people were taken to the old Eagledale ferry dock. The ferry *Kehloken* was to pick them up and take them to Seattle. Some of the children carried bunches of grass from their back yards to remind them of home. Where they were going, no grass grew. But they didn't know that yet.

Some white boys were there who had played hooky from school. They wanted to say goodbye to their classmates who were leaving. Some adults were there to say goodbye to their longtime neighbors. Some of the teenagers who were leaving wore the blue and gold sweaters of Bainbridge High School. Seven of the best players on the Bainbridge High baseball team were there. Half the team was being evacuated.

There was another sad parting at the ferry dock. Evaristo Arota was a Filipino and was married to a Japanese woman. He had to stay behind while his wife, Miki, was taken away.

The soldiers formed the people into line. There was absolute silence as they walked aboard the ferry in single file. Some of the small children

Posting the Order

MOHAI P-I 28035

Japanese American families were given eight days to leave their homes for evacuation to hastily built camps.

out over the roads of Bainbridge. The soldiers found most of the Japanese families waiting on their doorsteps with their luggage. They were allowed to take only the clothes and personal things they could carry. There were many sad partings. Children had to give up their pet dogs, cats, and chickens. One little girl had to leave her goat behind. Most of them found neighbors who would take care of their animals.

When Mr. and Mrs. Yosuke Moji climbed into the truck, their big Alaskan husky, King, jumped in with them. Two soldiers came up to pull him out, but King

He Wanted to Go, Too

When soldiers came for Mr. and Mrs. Yosuke Moji, King, their husky, jumped in the truck with them. Two men tried to remove him, but the dog snapped at them. Mrs. Moji, in tears, had to lead him back into the house where he watched them leave.

MOHAI P-I 28046

were skipping with delight. They were happy because they were going for a ride. But some of the older people had tears on their cheeks.

Then one little boy tripped and fell. He started to cry. As his mother tried to comfort him, other people started crying loudly. The soldiers were not used to seeing women and children in tears. They bit their lips and looked away to hide their own tears. Many people remember this as one of the saddest days in the history of Bainbridge Island.

BIHS 4482

Walt Woodward

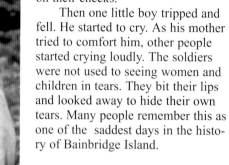

BIHS 4483

Milly Woodward

There were 227 men, women, and children aboard the train that took them to Manzanar, a hastily built camp in the high desert south of Bishop, California. Some Japanese residents moved away from the coast.

Some of the younger men were drafted or joined the Army while at the camp. Several served with the Army's most-decorated unit, the 442nd Regimental Combat Team. This all-Japanese-American unit played a decisive role in pushing the German Army out of Italy. Mo Nakata, Art Koura, and at least six other Bainbridge Islanders were wounded.

Other islanders who had good Japanese-language skills interrogated prisoners and served as translators of Japanese coded messages.

Day of Shame

Armed soldiers escort Japanese Americans along the Taylor Street dock in Eagledale to board a ferry March 29, 1942, en route to a "relocation" camp south of Bishop, California. Many islanders took a later ferry to see their neighbors board the train. The Associated Press sent this photo by a Seattle Post-Intelligencer *photographer to papers around the world.*

MOHAI P-I 28053

The Nakatas' First Market
*The Nakata family got its start in the market business
at the Eagle Harbor Market on Winslow Way.*

Town and Country
*Johnny Nakata waits on customers in the meat department of
Winslow's Town and Country Supermarket, which opened
in 1957, a joint venture of the Nakata and Loverich families.*

In December 1944, the government, finally admitting that the country's Japanese residents and their American-born children posed no threat, announced it was going to shut down the camps and let the Japanese return to their homes.

But on Bainbridge Island and in some other communities, groups denounced the action and urged that the Japanese not be allowed to come back. Several islanders held a meeting to oppose the Japanese islanders' return. Walt Woodward, who attended, criticizing their racist stand. Milly wrote a page-one story about the meeting for the *Review,* quoting her husband and other participants at length.

Only about half of the Japanese who had lived on the island did return. Many who did had to start over. Others, with the help of island friends, had been able to retain their land, and they began farming again. But old friendships remained strong despite the long separation.

"Most of the real islanders welcomed the Japanese back at the end of the war," the minority history report says. "Businessmen picked up where they left off. Mo Nakata and Ed Loverich leased Bainbridge Gardens from Mr. Seko and Mr. Harui."

Mo became manager of the meat counter at the store they built in

Island Center. Johnny Nakata bought the Eagle Harbor Market in 1952. In 1957, the three of them built the Town and Country Supermarket in Winslow. Several years later, through the efforts of Don Nakata and the other partners, they added new markets in Poulsbo and other communities.

In 1958, Junkoh and Chris Harui started a flower shop adjacent to the new supermarket and later moved to the corner of Highway 305 and High School Road, expanding to include gardening supplies.

In 1989, the Haruis reopened Bainbridge Gardens at Island Center. Completing the circle of life, they also built a Japanese garden near the pine trees his father had planted half a century earlier. It has become a gardening and gathering place for people throughout the region.

Agate Pass Bridge Gets Its Buttresses

*During the summer of 1949, construction crews had to hustle to get the new bridge's foundations in before the rainy season.
Construction was completed in sixteen months, ending forever Bainbridge Island's separation from the greater United States.*

Chapter Twenty-One

The Bridge

For at least ten thousand years, the island we call Bainbridge existed as a land apart, a retreat from the bustle of communities on the mainland. Then came The Bridge.

By Douglas Crist
Editor, *Bainbridge Island Review*

You just can't say "sink the ferry" without its complementary refrain: "And blow up the bridge."

The double-barreled mantra of island isolationism—a little wishful, a little wistful—can still be heard passing local lips, usually when afternoon traffic backs up on the highway, or a new subdivision takes root down the road. Wouldn't it be nice, local nostalgiacs wax, if we could go back to a time when there weren't so many of us here? When, perhaps, there was no bridge?

'Twasn't always so. Time was when islanders saw their economic prospects directly tied to the Kitsap Peninsula. What constituted cross-island traffic in those days followed the rutted tracks connecting our various ferry docks. Road maintenance, like pothole avoidance, was hit-or-miss.

Islanders had also long been subjected to the service and pricing whims of private Mosquito Fleet ferries. A bridge was seen not just as a vital link west; ease of vehicle travel, it was argued, would have a moderating influence on ferry fares around the sound. Build a bridge? Why not! And throw in a new highway, too!

Nobody worried much about who might move here, or what they might build. There was, after

BIHS

First Shovel
Governor Arthur Langlie turned over the symbolic first shovelful of earth for the Agate Pass Bridge on May 25, 1949.

all, no shortage of land with a population that numbered just a few thousand. A direct connection to the mainland would bring more people, more money, more commerce and trade.

So Bainbridge folk didn't just want a bridge to reach their mainland kin, they demanded one. Maybe even two.

It's doubtful that history honors the islander who, at a town meeting or perhaps the local tavern, first proposed a bridge to the Kitsap Peninsula. What is known is that by the late 1920s, the cause had been taken up by a fledgling Bainbridge Chamber of Commerce and by the local newspaper.

Their calls eventually brought the issue to the attention of Olympia. In its May 5, 1932, edition, the *Review* reported that state highway director Samuel Humes visited the island with a cadre of engineers in tow.

The Legislature had appropriated $10,000 for survey of a road connecting Port Blakely with Agate Passage; it was hoped that more money would be forthcoming for construction not just of that road but also a bridge, said by the newspaper to be "one of the great aims of Bainbridge folks."

"The visitors paid the *Review* a call," the editor wrote of the highway officials' sojourn, "and are always welcome. Come again."

But little happened for the next five years, and island life meandered on in relative remoteness. Mosquito Fleet routes linked Winslow and Eagledale with downtown Seattle, and the west side of the island with Brownsville and later

Inspection Crew
The bridge site became a major local tourist attraction.

BIHS 4534

On June 9, 1944, *Review* editor Walt Woodward opined:

"Frankly, we are getting a little bored with would-be politicians working us for some free publicity . . . with the pre-ballot pronouncement that 'If elected, I will work for the Agate Pass Bridge.' Politicians have been pulling that vote-getting wheeze since shortly after old Cap'n Vancouver dropped hook off Restoration Point."

Islanders rejoiced when, in July 1947, Democratic Gov. Mon Wallgren announced that construction of the Agate Passage Bridge was "No. 1" on the state's list of projects. The bridge, then envisioned as a four-lane affair, was estimated at $1.45 million; construction would be under the auspices of the Washington Toll Bridge Authority, with costs to be recovered through a toll on wayfarers.

Local elation was short-lived. In mid-1948, Wallgren announced his intention to scuttle the bridge in favor of a floating span linking Fletcher Bay with Manette. After a frantic meeting by Winslow town leaders, the commissioners of seven surrounding counties were entreated to sign a resolution urging Wallgren "to get along with construction" at Agate Passage.

Their fears were assuaged when the U.S. Army, which had permitting authority over bridges spanning navigable waters, said it had never heard of Wallgren's floating brainstorm.

Bremerton. But the arrangement could be inconvenient, as in 1935 when a 33-day ferry strike left islanders stranded. Finally in 1937, a survey by engineers led the State Good Roads Association to declare a bridge necessary and the appropriate location to be Agate Passage, presumably because it represented the shortest distance between island and peninsula.

In 1940, the state Legislature approved construction of the bridge, but failed to earmark any funds for the project. And for the next five years, island, state and country found themselves preoccupied by more pressing matters overseas. It was not until World War II ended that the bridge proposal resurfaced. Yet the record suggests that Washington pols were fairly shameless in flashing the idea to court the island vote.

200

Millie Heeney

Water View
A boater caught the bridge as it reached the passage's midpoint.

The governor wasn't done, though, and next tied the bridge to state acquisition of the Mosquito Fleet. Wallgren reasoned that bond funding could more easily be secured if the projects were lumped together. That brought more protests from Bainbridge Island, and public acquisition of the ferry system turned into one of the major issues in the governor's re-election bid that fall. At the same time, with bridge construction seeming closer at hand, attention turned to the question of just how to get to it.

Proposals for a limited-access "freeway" from Agate Passage to Rolling Bay were drawn up, but snagged when the Seabold Community Club objected to construction through their neighborhood. After several town meetings, citizens there voted 36-12 to endorse the plan. Seabold resident John C. Ralson summed up the sentiments of the day, saying, "Our quiet community is passing. A real highway is needed to handle traffic. . . ."

The contract for bridge construction was finally awarded to the Manson Construction and Engineering Company of Seattle. Wallgren, though, would not be around to hail its completion—or even the groundbreaking. He lost the *Review's* endorsement and then the election, bested in November 1948 by Republican challenger Arthur B. Langlie. The governor-elect wasted no time assuming the mantle of

bridge-builder. Two weeks after defeating Wallgren, Langlie sent emissaries to a community dinner at the Rolling Bay Grange Hall, with promises that construction would get under way as soon as the governor took office. And if that wasn't soon enough, he vowed, a temporary floating bridge would precede it. It never came to that, as right of way had already been acquired and land cleared on each side of the water. A ceremonial spade-turning was observed on May 25, 1949, inspiring 250 islanders to "drive or tramp across dusty roads" to the site for the sun-baked afternoon event. Governor Langlie himself headed the list of dignitaries on hand. At the podium, he hailed the bridge as "the new key" to the Puget Sound highway system.

The bridge, finally, was under way. In fact, the *Review* noted, "The ceremony meant no cessation of work for the 50 construction workers. A huge floating crane continued to operate during the speeches, and a hoarse whistle from a piece of construction equipment punctuated one of the governor's remarks."

On an otherwise celebratory occasion, though, islanders were taken somewhat aback by an ominous comment by Seattle Mayor

William F. Devin—words that curiously presaged the sentiments of future decades. Said Devin: "I formerly lived here and loved Bainbridge Island without a bridge. I am going to see if I love Bainbridge Island as much with a bridge."

Expected to be completed within 14 months, construction of the Agate Passage Bridge ran long by about 60 days. That gave islanders more time to wonder: If one bridge is good, wouldn't two be better? Talk of a once-proposed link to Bremerton was revived, however briefly; the governor himself predicted that, within a decade, a series of new bridges would cross Puget Sound itself.

Meanwhile, back at Agate Passage, the long-coveted first span took shape. Giant concrete abutments rose up from the water, across which were fitted a latticework of steel trusses in a lazy arc. The first islanders to cross the bridge did so surreptitiously—heedless of the 75-foot drop to the water below, eight boys tight-roped across the girders and a skeleton of planking in early July. The young daredevils were admonished by the newspaper, but a few weeks later, three island men undertook the same crossing in an effort to cut down on travel time to a meeting in Port Gamble. Their journey was chronicled by a witness in the *North Kitsap Herald:*

"The daylight crossing late Thursday afternoon proved interesting. Going back at 11:30 p.m. was more interesting, with no moonlight to augment the two flashlights of the three pilgrims as they headed eastward over the span. The last we saw of the three, they were silently and gingerly trodding the narrow plankway into the awesomely dark canyon of steel, each quietly reminding the other not to misstep. . . ."

The big day finally arrived on Oct. 7, 1950. A crowd of several thousand gathered for the opening ceremonies, which included a cannon salute and a water pageant staged by fourteen local yacht clubs. Dignitaries came from around the state and from as far away as Victoria, B.C. The bridge—two lanes, 1,229 feet in length, built for $1.398 million plus interest, but not yet painted—was hailed by state highway director W. A. Bugge as "strong and sure . . . a thing of beauty," to the approval of those assembled. Then, at exactly 3:34 p.m., a giant wooden key was fitted into a like-sized lock that dangled across the lanes, a symbolic opening of the peninsula beyond to direct motor access by islanders and those from points further east.

The assembled motorists—2,000 strong, plus another 1,000 or so who had mistakenly been told to wait in their cars some distance away and thus missed the ceremonies—began a steady, wheeled crawl across the bridge.

Ninety minutes later, islanders were still streaming across bumper to bumper (a portent of what would become, decades later). The first islanders to open their coin purse at the Suquamish-end tollbooth were Mr. and Mrs. Art Ganson, although several folks coming the other direction had earned that dubious honor a few moments earlier.

The celebration was linked to the grand opening of an improved Winslow ferry terminal ("New . . . Modern . . . Built for the Future!" as it was billed in a newspaper advertisement), where an evening dance attracted 1,500 people. Many celebrants also made their way to a giant clambake (2,000 pounds were steamed, in two open pits) on the Suquamish waterfront, behind which the bridge towered as a majestic backdrop. The day's most conspicuous no-show turned out to be Governor Langlie himself, who a week earlier had announced that, for unspecified reasons, he would be unable to attend. In his next editorial, Woodward noted Langlie's absence in unflattering terms and, rather than thanking the governor for the bridge's completion, proceeded to flay him for the sorry condition of the roadways at either end.

"The *Review* hopes that this winter's traffic toll on those death-trap thoroughfares will not be too great," Woodward wrote. Still, he conceded, "it would be in error to overlook the simple greatness of 'our' bridge."

In any event, after a quarter-century of dashed island hopes, the bridge was an immediate success. Nearly 10,500 people crossed the span in its first four days, generating $1,634.36 in tollbooth revenue. Traffic trailed off after a few days, as the locals settled into a pattern of normal use—567 persons crossed the following Monday, and 574 on Tuesday, for two-day revenues of $259.51.

The first signs of a long-desired commercial linkage between island and peninsula turned up in newspaper advertisements. Poulsbo merchants welcomed Bainbridge customers, while a Bremerton-area drive-in theater sought to lure island motorists over for the evening. ("Comfort and privacy in your own car! Lunch and smoke in your car!" patrons were bade. The fare that week included Barbara Stanwyck in "The Furies" and Gary Cooper in "The Gunfighter.")

Of course, the bridge also worked in reverse. Ferry operators noted an upsurge in business on the Winslow run—North Kitsap residents began to abandon the Suquamish-Seattle route, carpooling across the

Ready for Business

Drivers had to pay a five-cent toll to use the new bridge, but traffic was so sparse the state canceled the toll less than a year later.

island to take advantage of the more regular service here.

"They have found that if they take a ferry from Winslow," one captain reported, "they can sleep an hour later in the morning."

The toll lasted less than a year. Traffic has increased a bit, with 20,000 cars now crossing the span each day, and it periodically gets a new coat of paint. Other than that, it remains generally unchanged since its debut in 1950.

For its architectural significance and impact on regional growth and transportation (Seattle-Suquamish ferry service ended almost overnight), the bridge was added to state and national historic registers in 1995. Other, bigger bridges predicted to cross Puget Sound never did materialize, nor did the span to Bremerton.

In their absence developed a certain local isolationism—Bainbridge as refuge—with the bridge symbolic less of the opportunities it presents than the annoyances—traffic, noise, newcomers—it brings.

Walt Woodward may have foreseen as much, arguing in 1944 that islanders ought to consider how their community might develop without a link to their mainland kin.

At stake, he wrote, was "whether (Bainbridge) really will be part of Kitsap County, or whether it likes the idea of being an orphan stuck out in Puget Sound with neither Kitsap County nor King County's Seattle giving a whoop whether we sink or swim."

Orphans, it seems, we now would be content to remain.

—Reprinted with permission of the *Bainbridge Island Review*

Bibliography

Ambrose, Stephen E. *D-DAY June 6, 1944: The Climactic Battle of World War II.* New York: Simon & Schuster, 1994.
—*Nothing Like It in the World, The Men Who Built the Transcontinental Railroad, 1863-1869.* New York: Simon & Schuster, 2000.

Bainbridge Island Review. "Century on the Harbor, Winslow 1890-1990." Bainbridge Island, Wash., Aug. 8, 1990.

Beach, Allen. *Bainbridge Landings.* Bainbridge Island: Driftwood Press, 1960, 1965, 1970.

Beal, Zoe M. *Bainbridge Island in Battened Buildings and Dipper Days.* Seattle: Dickson-Fletcher Printing, 1960.

Berg, A. Scott. *Lindbergh.* New York: G. P. Putnam's Sons, 1998.

Boorstin, Daniel J. *The Discoverers: A History of Man's Search to Know His World and Himself.* New York: Random House, 1983.

Bowden, Angie B. *Early Schools in Washington Territory.* Seattle: Lowman and Hanford, 1935.

Bowden, W. B. *Port Madison W. T.* Bainbridge Island: Port Madison Press, 1976.

Coman, Edwin T., Jr., and Helen M. Gibbs. *Time, Tide and Timber, Over a Century of Pope & Talbot.* Stanford University Press, 1949.

Cook, Warren L. *Flood Tide of Empire, Spain and the Pacific Northwest, 1543-1819.* New Haven and London: Yale University Press, 1973.

Crist, Douglas. "The Span of Time: How Bainbridge Got Its Bridge." *Bainbridge Island Review Almanac,* (2002): p. 11.

Crutchfield, James A. *It Happened in Washington.* Guilford, Conn.: Globe Pequot Press, 1999.

Doremus, Edward B. *Leaves from the Log of William Bainbridge.* Bainbridge Island: Privately published, 1996.

Drew, Peggy. *Company Town: Port Madison, Washington, 1854-1897.* Class paper, University of Washington 1994.

Duncan, Don. "Taming the Wild, Pre-statehood to 1900," *Seattle Times,* January 8, 1989.
—"Widening Horizons, 1900 to 1910," *Seattle Times*, February 12, 1989.

Elfendahl, Gerald W. *Streams of Bainbridge Island: Names, History, Folklore and Culture.* Bainbridge Island: Salmonberry Press, 1997.

Ficken, Robert E., and Charles P. LeWarne, *Washington: A Centennial History.* Seattle: University of Washington Press, 1988.

Fish, Harriet U. *Fish Tales of Port Gamble & Port Ludlow.* Privately published, Carlsborg, Wash.

Guttridge, Leonard F., and Jay D. Smith, *The Commodores.* New York: Harper & Row, 1969.

Hansen, Reid. "History from Crystal Springs," *Bainbridge Island Historical Society Newsletter,* January 1999.
—"World War II on Bainbridge Island," *Bainbridge Island Historical Society Newsletter,* Fall 2000.

Hays, Derek. *Historical Atlas of the Pacific Northwest.* Seattle: Sasquatch Books, 1999.

Henry, John Frazier. *Early Maritime Artists of the Pacific Northwest Coast, 1741-1841.* Seattle: University of Washington Press, 1984.

Jones, Nard. *Seattle.* Garden City, N.Y.: Doubleday & Co., 1972.

Kaylene, Anne T. *Judicially Murdered.* Scappoose, Ore.: Melton Publishing, 1999.

Kline, M. S., and G. A. Bayless. *Ferryboats: A Legend on Puget Sound.* Seattle: Bayless Books, 1983.

Kreisman, Lawrence. *The Bloedel Reserve: Gardens in the Forest.* Bainbridge Island: Arbor Fund, 1988.

Kushner, Peter Andrew. *Remembering, Forgetting, and Creating the Past: An analysis of how people assemble and understand the history of Port Madison.* Senior thesis, University of Washington, 1997.

Leahy, Colleen. "Bainbridge Island's Lynwood Center." Bremerton: *The Sun,* April 20, 1997.

Lee, Ivan W., Jr. *The Story of the Little Fort at Bean Point.* Bainbridge Island: Self-published, 1994.

Lindenberg, Charles W. *The Academy.* Kearny, Neb.: Morris Publishing, 1998.

Marriott, Elsie Frankland. *BAINBRIDGE through bifocals.* Seattle: Gateway Printing, 1941.

Meany, Edmond S. *Vancouver's Discovery of Puget Sound.* Portland, Ore.: Binfords and Mort, 1957.

Morgan, Murray. *Puget's Sound, A Narrative of Early Tacoma and the Southern Sound.* Seattle: University of Washington Press, 1979.
—*Skid Road, An Informal Portrait of Seattle.* Seattle: University of Washington Press, 1982.

Neal, Carolyn, and Thomas Kilday Janus. *Puget Sound Ferries: From Canoe to Catamaran.* Sun Valley, Calif.: American Historical Press, 2001.

Pelly, Thomas M., and G. C. Nickum. *The Story of Restoration Point and The Country Club.* Seattle: Lowman & Hanford, 1931.

Perry, Fredi. *Port Madison, Washington Territory , 1854-1889.* Bremerton: Perry Publishing, 1989.

Price, Andrew, Jr. *Port Blakely: The Community Captain Renton Built.* Seattle: Port Blakely Books, 1989.

Roberts, Brian, ed. *They Cast a Long Shadow: A History of the Nonwhite Races on Bainbridge Island.* Bainbridge Island, Wash.: Multicultural Advisory Council, Bainbridge Island School District 303, 1975.

Robinson, Greg. *FDR and the Internment of Japanese Americans.* Cambridge: Harvard University Press, 2001.

Smith, Phoebe. *80 Candles: A Collection of Life Stories.* Bainbridge Island, Wash.: Bainbridge Island Community Center, 1988.
—*Glimpses of Bainbridge: A Collection of Life Stories.* Bainbridge Island, Wash.: Bainbridge Island Community Center, 1992.

Smith, Toby. *The First Bainbridge Boom.* Monograph on Ports Madison and Blakely and Pleasant Beach. Bainbridge Island, Wash.

Stevens, Isaac I., *Explorations for a Route for a Pacific Railway,* Washington: Thomas H. Ford, 1860.

Vining, Dorothea. "Folks at Crystal Springs Always Have Taken Care of Themselves," *Bainbridge Review,* May 1963.

Ward, Andrew. "Haunted Home," *American Heritage,* July/August 1990, pp. 69-75.

Warner, Katy. *A History of Bainbridge Island.* Bainbridge Island, Wash.: Bainbridge Island Friends of the Library, 1968.
—"Katydids," columns in the *Bainbridge Review,* 1961-74.

Writers Program, WPA. *The New Washington, A Guide to the Evergreen State.* Portland, Ore.: Binfords & Mort, 1950.

Wilkes, Charles. *Narrative of the United States Exploring Expedition.* Philadelphia: Lea and Blanchard, 1845.

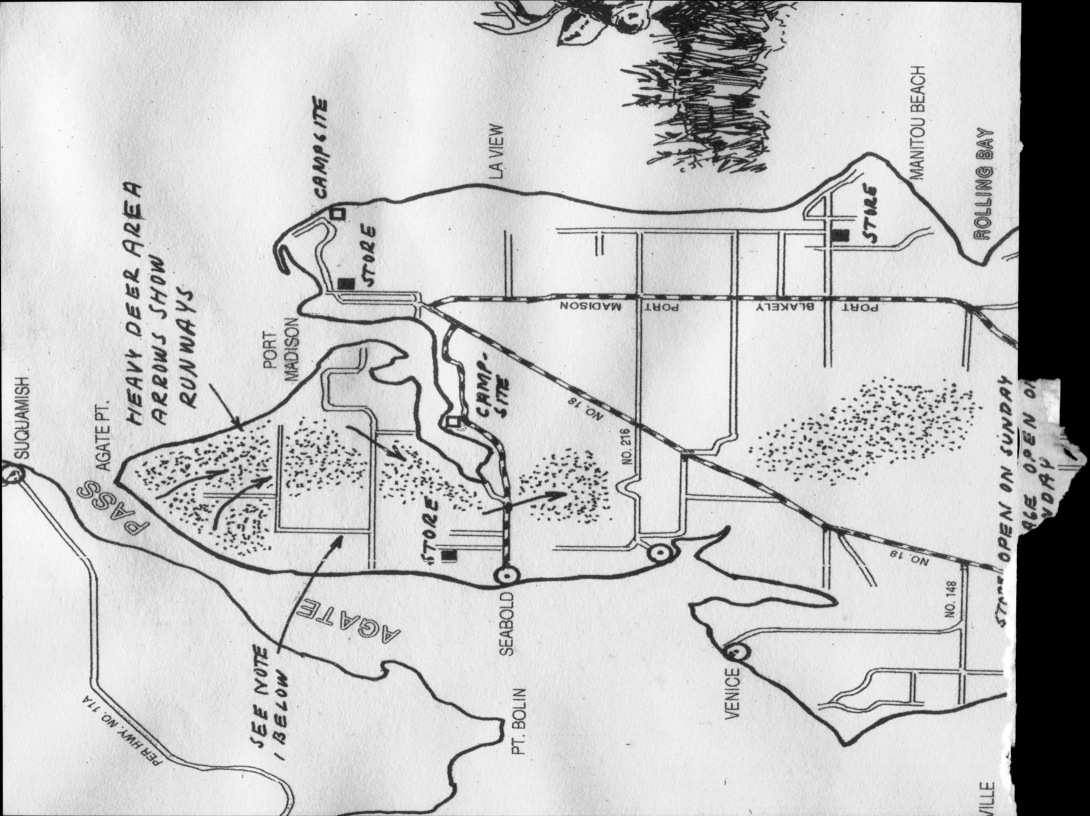